THE
LAST
THIRD
OF
LIFE
CLUB

THE LAST THIRD OF LIFE CLUB

JEROME ELLISON

A PILGRIM PRESS BOOK

from United Church Press, Philadelphia, Pennsylvania

Library of Congress Cataloging in Publication Data

Ellison, Earl Jerome, 1907—
    The Last Third of Life Club.

    "A Pilgrim Press book."
    Includes bibliographical references.
    1. Aged—United States. 2. Death—Psychology.
I. Title
HQ1064.U5E43   301.43'5'0973   73-13961
ISBN 0-8298-0252-5

The scripture quotations (unless otherwise indi-
cated) from the *Revised Standard Version of the
Bible*, copyrighted 1946 and 1952 by the Division of
Christian Education, National Council of Churches,
and are used by permission.

Excerpts from *Modern Man in Search of a Soul*
by Carl G. Jung are reprinted by permission of
Harcourt Brace Jovanovich, Inc.

United Church Press, 1505 Race Street,
Philadelphia, Pennsylvania 19102

CONTENTS

24027

INTRODUCTION

To describe how The Last Third of Life Club came into being is not a simple matter. Nobody "organized" or "founded" it. It seemed to be just there, preexisting. None of us did much more than acknowledge its existence and give it a name.

There have, of course, been individuals who made special contributions to this identifying process. Outstanding among these was the great Swiss psychiatrist Carl Jung. The central thoughts of The Last Third Club had been in circulation for many centuries before Jung. (This he frankly asserted; his candor in such matters is one of the reasons he can now be called "great.") But the way he so ably restated the matter in terms of twentieth-century science throws a strong new light on one of the most pressing problems of present-day society. It is called geriatrics by a science unable to impart meaning to the lives it prolongs and by younger people who would seek to deal from without with problems that can only be managed from within. Jung says that most people embark upon the second half of life wholly unprepared.

Are there perhaps colleges for forty-year-olds which prepare them for their coming life and its demands as the ordinary colleges introduce our young people to a knowledge of the world and of life? No, there are none. Thoroughly unprepared we take this step . . . with the false pre-supposition that our truths and ideals will serve us as hitherto. But we cannot live the afternoon of life according to the program of life's morning—for what was great in the morning will be little at evening, and what in the morning was true will at evening have become a lie. I have given psychological treatment to too many people of advancing years and looked too often into the secret chambers of their souls, not to be moved by this fundamental truth.[1]

Though we have not attempted to found the school for later living Dr. Jung proposed, what we have undertaken in this book may in many cases serve the same function. We quote him here not because he inspired us (many of us had never heard of him!) but because we know after the fact of our own hard-lived experience that what he says is true. For we are those who let our forties (and in most cases our fifties) slip by without preparing for the new life that presently descended upon us. Late in the game, after having seen many of our co-runners trip and fall in disaster, we paused and took stock. It was an eleventh-hour inventory, and it revealed many bare shelves. We were not prepared to do business in this new market. So we restocked.

By simply muddling through, we hit upon certain principles that seemed to work better than those which had served us so well during the first two thirds of life but miserably failed us now. By freaks of chance that sometimes seemed miraculous, we kept running into kindred spirits with whom we could share our experience. All seemed to have something to contribute to the project of living out the last third of life happily and creatively. At last we decided that the time had come to put the sum of our experience into some kind of readable form. The result is this book.

Having observed that wisdom bears no relation to academic credentials and that modern science has often erred, we have made proved and recent life experience our single criterion. What matters to us is not *who is right* but *what is true.* We respect an eminent Swiss, for example, not because he was a celebrated doctor but because what he said has checked out in our own lives.

On this same principle, we have adopted a policy of anonymity. We are moving forward into an expanding domain of little-explored reality. In these dimensions, to haggle over personal reputations and pet theories would be a waste of time we can't afford. We decided to be guided not by personal ambition but by results in human lives. Does this mean that we are impersonal and indifferent? Most certainly not. We are in every sense a club. Our membership includes specialists in many fields. The views of some of them appear—anonymously—in the appendix of this book. We hold regular meetings; this book is a sort of program guide for these meetings, where our concerns are the individual Jims and Joes, Janes and Pollys, who are concerned with the final third of life.

"A human being would certainly not grow to be seventy or eighty years old," wrote Dr. Jung, "if this longevity had no meaning for the species to which he belongs. The afternoon of human life . . . cannot be merely a pitiful appendage of life's morning." [2] We agree with Dr. Jung—and with the poet Robert Browning—that youth is not all but that "the best is yet to be." We are convinced we can prove this "best" to tens and perhaps hundreds of thousands who may be desperately seeking that release and relief now being enjoyed by our own relatively modest numbers. Longevity research indicates that, so long as one remains useful and sociable, living happily to be a hundred is no trick at all.

Jerome Ellison

Secretary, The Phenix Club
(Last Third Club of Guilford)
Box 25, Guilford, Connecticut 06437

Note: The Last Third Club has been renamed The Phenix Club. The new name is taken from the immemorial symbol of renewal and rebirth, the phenix.

ONE

We admit that death is closer for us who are in the last third of our lives than it is for the average person; that in this respect we are different from the majority of people.

We of The Last Third Club are a mixed assortment of human beings, in no way remarkable except for one thing—we no longer fear death.

Maybe even this is not very remarkable. For all we know there may be a great many people, possibly a majority, who have no fear of death. If this is the case, so be it. It would not change our conviction that something extraordinary and important has happened to us. For we are the people who once feared death a great deal—so much, in fact, that we wouldn't let ourselves talk about it or even think about it, sometimes covering our fear with a daredevil rashness intended to show that we had no fear! And yet we, these same people, now find ourselves fearing death less and less the closer we come to it.

This fact seems to us so remarkable, so unexpected, so altogether pleasing, so full of potential for shared happiness, that we are moved to set down our experiences in the hope that many others will share them and will let fall away from them, as it has fallen away from us, what had been a puzzling, ever-pressing, ever-depressing weight.

We once saw ourselves as having only a meager future, with even this remnant shrinking fast toward a vanishing point in a terrifying vacuum. Now we can face the future with an easy, sometimes even joyous confidence and serenity. Meanwhile our *present* lives— our lives in the immediate year—which once seemed

11

so sadly drained of future usefulness have taken on a new glow of meaning and potential. We find ourselves needed—and needed right away—by thousands if not millions of people.

The twelve-item capsule formulation of our experience that follows may appear to parallel certain redemptive movements of both the near and the remote past. This is intentional—some sort of brief summary of our experiences is essential—but any resemblance to other programs is only superficial. Our twelve conditions are not to be taken as a sequence, or a course of instruction, or creed. They are simply an attempt to set down, after the fact, some of the major states of mind that have come upon us—often seemingly spontaneously—and made us feel we have something important in common.

The sequence seems to mean little; these conditions may appear in any order. But we have noticed that where there is a strong tendency for any one of these things to develop in a particular life, sooner or later all twelve are likely to appear. We seem to have been set on a road that has twelve major access points. Some of us are far advanced on this highway; some have only recently set foot on it with a few tentative steps. It doesn't seem to matter very much. As we travel, our advance increases our confidence that we have found the path to a supremely desirable destination.

The first of the twelve conditions is stated at the opening of this chapter. Read it. At first it may seem to be an almost ridiculously simple statement of the obvious (closer examination will suggest another point of view.) Here are the others:

Two: We have come to see that, for those who are prepared, the eventual passage from this life can be a glory rather than a dread.

Three: We have decided to use our remaining years primarily for this preparation.

Four: We assert that the last third of life is given by nature for this high purpose; that it can illuminate all earlier experience in the joyous fulfillment of a rounded life.

Five: We have resolved to give over our lives to Cosmic Creative Intelligence as we individually name and experience this divine force.

Six: Through regular morning and evening meditations, we are finding ourselves more and more in harmony with this transcendent power.

Seven: Reviewing our past in the company of other Last Thirders has shown us that our earlier life goals no longer suffice.

Eight: Through reading, discussion, and reflection we have humbly attempted to discover and cultivate those higher values that are essential to our new life.

Nine: Having thus gained a clearer perspective on life's major phases, we have steadfastly sought the wisdom it is the business of life's later years to acquire and preserve.

Ten: These steps have brought an awareness of cosmic dimensions we had not hitherto explored and have led us into the realm of deep spiritual experience.

Eleven: Though aware that the workaday world undervalues spiritual wisdom, we offer what we have of it when asked.

Twelve: As our special responsibility, and as opportunity offers, we carry to others in the final third of life the heartening word that seniority can be joyous.

We now return for a closer look at Condition One: "We admit that death is closer for us who are in the last third of our lives than it is for the average person; that in this respect we are different from the majority of people." The action word here is "admit." Without it we have no more than a platitudinous restatement of something everybody already knows. We have all known for a long time that the physical body we have been taught is so important will some day wear out and be cast aside to be buried or burned. But knowing something intellectually is not the same as admitting it. The intellect can compartmentalize, keeping truth fragments in separate sealed boxes, along with such occasionally useful information as $A = \pi r^2$ or $2+2=4$. Thus separated, such "knowledge" may in no way affect the actual living of our lives. "Every one of us gladly turns away from his problems," Jung wrote;

if possible, they must not be mentioned, or, better still, their existence is denied. We wish to make our lives simple, certain and smooth—and for that reason problems are tabu. . . . Everything in us that still belongs to nature shrinks away from a problem; for its name is doubt, and wherever doubt holds sway . . . [we] are handed over to fear. . . . We choose to have certainties and no doubts . . . without even seeing that certainties can arise only through doubt . . . and results can only be brought about when we have ventured into and emerged again from the darkness. . . . The artful denial of a problem will not produce conviction; . . . a wider and higher consciousness is called for to give us the certainty and clarity we need.[1]

It would be hard to find a better statement of the situation we found ourselves in as we entered the last third of life. We were suddenly and uniquely beset with problems we could find no solution for. The economic system makes no secret of its eagerness to push us out of the way and give our places to younger people. Even when our knowledge and experience could save costly and painful mistakes, nobody wanted to listen to us. Sometimes they hardly waited till our backs were turned before smiling, winking, and wagging a finger in circular motion about the head. When they listened at all it was only with the brief patience traditionally allowed the dotard.

What we experienced inwardly did little to reassure us against the anxious signals we were receiving from outside. We aren't seeing, hearing, tasting, smelling, thinking, feeling, or remembering quite as well as we once did. We aren't as quick with tongue or feet, and we tire more easily. The effects of age are definitely upon us. It isn't the same as before when we were sick and then got well again and were as good as ever. We know some of the things wrong with us are never going to improve but will get steadily worse until finally, at some point in the not very distant future, they kill us. Death, that awful and mysterious thing we had heard about all our lives as a terrible but distant threat, is now near, actually reaching out its cold feelers to claim our bodies. And we cannot escape. What will come will come to us as it comes to everybody.

Even worse than the actual moment of our physical extinction, we dreaded the long, slow deterioration we had seen take so many before us—the loss of hair, teeth, eyes, and hearing; the inability to walk, talk, or care for bodily functions; the loss of clarity of mind and memory; the general incompetence of living, the sinking to a vegetable level from which death would be a welcome deliverance. Terrified, we sought refuge in a hundred varieties of escape and denial. As Jung saw, "many old people prefer to become hypochondriacs, niggards, doctrinaires, applauders of the past or eternal adolescents," [2] we observed in ourselves and our contemporaries these and dozens of other symptoms of fearful flight from this new challenge life was now offering us—the challenge of rising to meet death fearlessly and creatively. Some of us solved the problem by simply taking to the bottle and drinking ourselves to death. Others committed suicide by the quicker means of firearms, "accidents," or depressant drugs. Others expressed their denial in ways less somber but just as ridiculous, by pretending they were immune to the defects of age. Thus we had our seventy-year-old woman behaving as she did when she was a cute seven-year-old, "Daddy's little girl in pigtails"; our eighty-year-old dandy marrying his twenty-year-old secretary to show he was just as sharp a fellow with the girls as he was two thirds of a century earlier; our overage corporation executive hanging onto his job of making money he didn't know what to do with just to prove he was as good a money-maker as ever. Others, the hypochondriacs among us, were less outright in our denial; we conceded that age was approaching but figured we could ward it off by barricading ourselves behind a fortress of pill bottles, dietary foods, and athletic regimens. Some of the less lethal of these devices seemed to work for a time, but all of them in the end wore thin and broke down. Those of us who remained were forced to conclude that denial was not the answer.

A few of us hit on the idea that, since denial hadn't worked, we might try its opposite—affirmation. Instead of telling ourselves we weren't showing any marked effects of aging, we began to own up to the fact that we were. Instead of pretending that we weren't really going to die very soon, we began to concede that our time was not so far off. Instead of pretending that we were just the same as the younger elements of the population, we began to accept the circumstance that in important ways we were different. Instead of rating youth as the "prime" of life, we cast aside the youth cult and its propaganda, in which we had been immersed all our lives, seeing youth as only one of several transitory phases of a complete life cycle and age as the culmination that gives both youth and age their meaning and fulfillment. Instead of fearing death as an ignoble end, we began to see that meeting it with serenity, courage, resourcefulness, and skill provides that crowning challenge of the fully lived life.

The results astonished us. Only when we gave them up did we begin to realize what a price in energy-expenditure the maintenance of our denial mechanisms had been exacting, what an enormous effort it is to try to live a lie. We took up with a will our therapy of affirmation. Yes, we were getting older and feebler. Yes, we would die statistically sooner than the younger elements of the population. Yes, we might be sick for a while before we died.

For some of us, these admissions were not easy at first. To admit is not the same as shallow intellectual acknowledgment. To admit is to "let in," to take into the very structure of our being the same facts we had taken such exhausting pains to keep out. Some of us, by misuse of the divine gift of human imagination, put ourselves through an agonizing period of imagined horrors before winning the ability to accept with equanimity the idea that the simple facts of life and death applied to ourselves as well as to others.

Only those old enough to have lived through it can know how hard this can be—or how much the moral support of others in the last third of life can mean during this crisis. But we found that if we stuck with it, and utilized all available supports, we would win through to a point where we could calmly (or with only brief moments of panic!) consider our approaching death as one of the ordinary facts of life. Our fears diminished to a point where they stimulated rather than inhibited constructive action.

And now some amazing things began to happen. As the energy we had been pouring into denial mechanisms was released, new resources of mental, physical, and emotional vigor came pouring into us. We were almost "ourselves" again. As we directed our imaginative powers away from morbidity, they took hold of the problems of the last third of life with surprising skill. Answers to formerly unanswerable problems began to appear, sometimes with unexpected ease. Were our physical and mental powers diminished? Very well, we'd put to the best possible use whatever was left of them. Were we going to die before long? Then we'd better pull ourselves together to do a good job of it. As we began to look around with open eyes, we found worlds of resources opening to us we had never known existed. Why, the last third of life might be a really splendid thing! With a new will, we began to explore life's new possibilities.

TWO

We have come to see that, for those who are prepared, the eventual passage from this life can be a glory rather than a dread.

The important thing to notice about this condition is its tentative nature. In this phase we are not absolutely cocksure about anything, so the phrasing of the step is conditional. We don't assert that everybody can experience a blissful death but only "those who are prepared." We don't claim that they *will* but that they "can." We don't say that the thing is obvious or easy; we have only gradually "come to see." The distinguishing feature of Condition Two is an open mind, a willingness to entertain new evidence on propositions once perhaps regarded as doubtful, a readiness to put to energetic work some unused portions of our minds.

The famous British author H. G. Wells thoroughly understood Condition Two. At his deathbed, friends and relatives were hovering about trying to make comforting sounds. He asked them to go away and added, "Can't you see I'm busy dying?"

Busy dying! Wells, one of the enlightened men of his time—educated, informed, and wise—knew he was on the point of death. He also quite evidently knew the difference between "those who are prepared" and those who are not. He had discovered certain details of his preparation for the most important task of that phase of his life—doing a good job of dying—that still had not been accomplished to his satisfaction. And so, right up to the moment of his passing, he was "busy."

Busy at what? Of course we cannot say specifically.

But from our own experience we believe we can form a fairly good notion of the *kind* of thing that occupied his mind. It was the same kind of thing that now occupies ours, the readjustment of certain generally accepted ideas inculcated during the first two thirds of life to the realities of the last third. Foremost among these reassessment jobs is to make clear to our everyday minds the difference between *self-preservation* and *self-realization*.

For a time it looked as though the well-advertised instinct of self-preservation might become the bogey of our later years. All our lives, any threat to our bodies had brought an instant and energetic response of what we have been calling the self-preservation instinct. If we were beaten as children ("for our own good," of course!), we were imprinted with a fear of bodily annihilation and marked for life with a tense mistrust of anybody capable of showing hostility. We were eternally on guard against any possibility of bodily harm. Even if raised by gentle parents, our natural instinct was reinforced by constant admonitions to "take care of ourselves"—that is, take care of our bodies. Our early and middle years carried a heavy load of warnings against this or that contagion, accident hazard, economic risk, or injury to eye, lung, foot, ear, stomach, or tooth. Our medicine cabinets were likely to be stuffed with pills, lotions, and potions we believed will strengthen and protect our bodies. The drug-advertising industry does all it can to drive us to hypochondria. Some of us were well on our way even in our early years, so powerful was the social reinforcement of a natural protective tendency.

In our later years this anxiety to protect ourselves became more pronounced. The knowledge that death is statistically much closer to us than it has ever been before acts as a trigger to our self-protective drives. Even the *thought* of death may send us compulsively reaching for our pills and other reassurances. Have we taken our vitamins and our blood-pressure, allergy, nerve, and kidney medicines? Are the rent, light, heat, grocery, insurance, and doctor bills all paid? Will our pension, dividend, interest, or social security check be on time? Is that funny feeling we have in the arm just a harmless twitch or is it something really serious? If we have children, our egos may extend the perimeter of our anxieties to include them. Are they doing well in all respects? Are we still in the good graces of our men and women friends and relatives? If all these matters are in good shape we may extend our outer defenses even farther, to include our favorite corporation, our political party, our country. In extreme cases, there is no limit to the things we take into account as essential for our peace of mind. Anxieties over them sometimes make life all but unbearable.

This same "unbearable" condition finally forced some of us to do some thinking and investigating. Clearly, it was a futile game to bring yourself to the brink of nervous exhaustion trying to protect something you would eventually lose anyway. What was this body we were at such pains to defend? When we looked into the business, we found that physiologically it was only the most recent of a long sequence of bodies we had occupied, used, and discarded. There had been a fetus body, a baby body, an infant body, a child body, preadolescent, adolescent, and postadolescent bodies, and several adult-body replacements. The body we now inhabited, like all the others, was in a constant state of disintegration and repair. To "preserve" it, at the urging of a presumed instinct for self-preservation or any other agency, was an impossibility. We were lost, therefore, so long as we were centered on body preservation.

We began to ask what forces lie behind, beyond, and above the body. Obviously, since we continued an uninterrupted existence through a whole range of bodies, there was something other than a body, *something not solely physical*. What force is resident in us that is able continually to create and discard bodies? By pursuing this question, we arrived at a well-developed concept of Self.

What we learned about the Self struck us at first as a piquant combination of the familiar and the strange, the old and the new. At first, Self sounded a little like the "soul" they used to tell us about in church (which some of us had long since stopped attending). Those of us who had become interested in comparing religions were able to point out resemblances to the Self of the Bhagavad Gita, written in India more than five thousand years ago. But the Self set forth in our time is expounded under auspices neither ancient nor religious. Names such as Carl Jung and Abraham H. Maslow figured prominently in formulating the contemporary concept of Self, the former a pioneer and co-founder of twentieth-century psychiatry; the latter, right into the 1970s, chairman of psychology at one of our leading universities and former president of the professional society of U.S. psychologists, the American Psychological Association. From here and from there, we were able to piece together a fairly good layman's working idea of Self. It came to this:

The Self is the creative center within us. In its normal or unrealized state it resides in the unconscious—that is, in that part of our total psyche that is not readily accessible to our workaday minds. The Self is the great general organizing power within us, mainly mental and spiritual in substance but having a direct supervisory concern and authority in psychophysiological processes. It can appropriate molecules and energies and utilize them to its purposes. It is aware of dimensions not readily experienced by our workaday minds. It stimulates those minds to evolutionary growth. It is able to create bodies suitable to our world situation and sees to the discard of bodies no longer appropriate. The Self is cosmic. It knows itself in relation to all time and all creation—to the cosmos. Thus "Self-realization"—those times when the gates between conscious and deep unconscious are fully opened and the Self is made known to the workaday intellect—is experienced as supernatural joy and bliss, a direct contact with that which has direct contact with the divine.

In religious terms this is "the kingdom of heaven that is within you," "the pearl of great price, worth selling all that you have to possess," the "Inner Light." Maslow, a scientist and hence not one to invoke solely religious authority, has said that Self-realization is the pinnacle ("peak") of mature living. Jung, without specifically saying so, hints that Self may survive death with memory, recognition, and a continued—perhaps even greatly accelerated—will to live and achieve. Many distinguished psychic researchers, from the great Englishman Frederic W. H. Myers to the contemporary U.S. professors H. M. DuCasse and Gardner Murphy, state categorically that the Self's survival of death is a fact. Death, they insist, does not impede the Self's function of making bodies. But when the individual progresses from the gross physical heaviness of the obstructed universe to the finer-woven, more purely mental realms, it requires a body made of finer, more penetrating stuff. And so the Self creates a new, more appropriate, more ethereal body. It seems likely that this is what H. G. Wells, in full Self-realization at the time of his transition, found himself "busy" doing.

All this, of course, is far beyond where we find ourselves while in Condition Two. Nevertheless, the mere open-minded acknowledgment of the possibility of such things, even if we regarded them as still un-proved, carried us measurably closer to the condition of "coming to see" that, for those who are prepared, the eventual passage from this life could be a glory rather than a dread.

We next turned our attention from our future death to our present life. If there was indeed a radiant, joy-filled center within us, and if its realization was indeed the pinnacle, the goal, the purpose, and the fulfillment of life on earth, we certainly should waste no more time in getting to know this center. We didn't have to wait till we were on the point of death; if happy Self-realization turned out to be available now, it surely would be available then. Accordingly, we turned our minds to our *present* stock-in-trade.

As we contemplated the subject, we began to realize that we had already experienced intimations of Self. These may have come while walking under the moon or beside a river or along a deserted beach or across a flowered meadow, or while watching a water-fall, a grate fire, or a storm, or while sitting in church, or being in a far place, or in love, or alone, or while studying poems, or snowflakes, or small things like butterflies, or big things like galaxies. But come they had. Within reach of our memory had come those moments of the total, blissful relatedness that is the hallmark of the Self.

At the time, perhaps, we have paid little attention. Afterward, we were inclined to discount the experience as simply a few moments of "feeling good" (*unusually* good!) but no more. Now, however, these recollected moments took on a new meaning. Their source, we came to realize, was the Self. It was a source inexhaustible once tapped, an unending, bound-lessly flowing river of well-being. There began to be born in us a desire to reach and realize that source on some more dependable, permanent basis. And this was for the immediate here and now, not alone for some uncertain and hypothetical future moment of passage.

We did not, however, make any attempt to put out of our minds the fact that death was coming closer to us with each revolution of the clock. We kept our minds continually open to further evidence on this point and found testimony steadily accumulating that joy in the hour of passing was a real possibility. Some of our contemporaries had experienced long comas during illnesses that had carried them to the very door of death; a few had even been pronounced dead by medical authority. And most of these people had brought back tales of an unearthly joy as the threshold of transition was approached. In addition, when some of our friends had permanently passed over, a few had done so with attitudes and facial expressions unmistakably reflecting an inner joy. The more hard-nosed among us fell back on the Socratic position. If death is nothing but a final going to sleep, Socrates said, he'd welcome it as a well-earned and much-needed rest. If it should turn out that death was a passage to another and happier phase of life, that too would be welcome. And so, whether by Socratic or Self-realization insights, we made ourselves receptive to the whole range of creative attitudes toward the final third of our earth lives and our eventual departure.

There remained our institutionalized terrors of illness and destitution. But these terrors gradually began to fade as entirely new horizons steadily opened before us; we'd been sick and broke before; the Self had survived and could do so again if necessary. It didn't greatly matter. Other and far more interesting possibilities were now occupying our thoughts.

Thus we arrived at Condition Two. We had "come to see that, for those who are prepared, the eventual passage from this life can be a glory rather than a dread." Now, with an open mind toward still unheard-of possibilities, and with a new hope and excitement, we were prepared to accept the philosophical challenge specifically reserved for the last third of life: the quest for the great truths of life and of death.

THREE

We have decided to use our remaining years primarily for this preparation.

Condition Three works a definite change of emphasis. Having made at least a temporary peace with the fact of death, we now swing our attention single-pointedly to the fact of life. We're not dead yet by a long shot. There may be many years still at our disposal. What shall we do with them?

The action word in Number Three is "decided." We're going to make a decision, a final choice, one that will hold for the rest of our lives. We have decided on "preparation." What, exactly, does this involve?

To prepare means to get ready, and how you prepare depends upon what you're getting ready for. If it's a fight you do your roadwork, if it's an examination you study, and so on. Death, so far as we could find out, was a combination physical-mental-spiritual event. Physically we couldn't see much to do beyond what we were already doing—that is, taking reasonable care that our death be not premature. Spiritually involved metaphysics, and we were not yet ready for that. So we decided to zero in on the third aspect, the mental one.

We had always known we were mentally unprepared to face death, but there had always seemed to be more immediate things to think about. A person with children to feed, bills to pay, or a career to build doesn't have much time, we had said, to prepare his mind on the subject of death. But now the children were grown and gone, our bills were more or less budgeted to our income, we'd already had whatever career we might reasonably expect, and there was no further excuse for delaying this preparation.

Almost at once we made a most humiliating discovery. Not only were we deficient in our knowledge of death, we knew practically nothing about life. What was it for? How big was the universe and where was it heading? It would seem a shame to leave this physical sphere before we had taken a more careful look at it. We decided to learn about life—not *all* about it, of course (we couldn't do that even with an entire unspent lifetime before us), but enough to give us a reasonably secure adjustment to the general configuration of things.

The stellar universe, for example, once we let ourselves be really aware of it, gave us a new perspective on the setting of which we ourselves are a part, not in shadowy, mystical terms but in the straight linear space and ordinary clock time to which our minds had long been accustomed. Simple, popular, easy-to-read books (see reviews in Appendixes) stated the case for us in plain language. Familiar everyday things, long taken for granted and not really observed, began to arouse a new wonder. The sun's rays that beat warm on our foreheads at noon, we learned, had left the sun exactly five hundred seconds earlier and had been traveling toward us at what is thought to be top speed allowed any energy particle in the physical universe—186,000 miles a second.

When we let this idea sink in, it became more than another interesting fact. We were in actual *living relationship* with this fiery ball whose rays reached us just eight minutes and twenty seconds after they left their source. Our earthly existence was totally dependent on its life-giving emanations and the subsidiary earth cycles (nitrogen cycle, water cycle, protein cycle, etc.) they engender. Our radius of awareness was suddenly extended by ninety-three million miles!

The word transcendence took on new meaning. Hitherto, this word had designated no more than a hazy poetic reaching for what is above and beyond, having little to do with practical reality. But with sun consciousness dawned an awareness that everything we had regarded as immediate and practical was totally dependent on what was above and beyond. We were citizens not only of a city, a state, and a nation but also of a planet, a stellar system, a galaxy, and a cosmos.

While looking skyward, we reflected that the moon and the sun rule the tides and that there are tides in all fluids, including glandular ones; cycles of the moon are reflected in cycles of human moods and activities. Moonless nights, even more instructive, gave us our first clear experience of our direct relatedness to the wonders of the deep sky. A few of us bought small telescopes for such excitements as the mountains of the moon, the cloud bands of Jupiter and his ever-shifting moons, the rings of Saturn and *his* moons, the jewellike radiance of the trapezium in the Orion nebula. The greatest night-sky wonder of all, the Andromeda nebula, comes free to the unaided eye. Here, a million and a half light-years beyond the great star clouds of our own Milky Way nebula floats another great spiral of star clouds almost exactly its size—two hundred light-years across and twenty deep.

Here, in perceiving space-time phenomena that infinitely transcend any conceivable physical lifetime, was transcendence indeed! We were in direct visual touch with objects incredibly distant, seeing a nebula as it was a million and half years ago. It was a fitting introduction to transcendence, the thing that would become the most important single activity of the last part of our lives. What we were to experience at death would *transcend* anything we had ever known before; the more familiar we were with the principle of transcendence, the better prepared we'd be.

The main obstacle to successful transcendence is adherence to our habitual mundane thought patterns. We must begin to make our separation from these now. It will not be easy. There always seems to be some leftover business from the first half of life. Much of it falls into the "I've always wanted to" category. Some of it involves expressing parts of our personality hitherto submerged. Dr. Jung, who gave the matter much thought, saw a frequent reversal of traditional masculine-feminine interests during the later years. This, he said, allowed the latent "feminine side" of men to be expressed and vice versa. Thus a businessman known in his early years as a hard driver, go-getter, self-starter, and money-maker may in his retirement become a stay-at-home interested mainly in easel painting and cookery. (World War II Admiral Chester W. Nimitz declared on his retirement that he intended to become a baby-sittter!) On the other side of the sex equation, many women who spent the first half of their lives in quiet domestic pursuits have, in their later years, burst into successful business activity, commanding enterprises ranging from gift shops, bakeries, and delicatessens to trucking firms and steam-engine factories.

One of the mass phenomena of our time is the hordes of aging persons trouping about the world on package tours, working out the "I've-always-wanted-to-travel" urge. An enormous and sometimes spectacular creativity (such as that of Grandma Moses) may result from these long-denied and finally expressed urges— "I've always wanted to paint" (or play the piano, or hike, or sing, or sculpt, or be psychoanalyzed). These leftover urges may also take a destructive turn. One successful businessman who had been a teetotaler into his fifties abruptly decided his life had not contained enough carousing, and in four flaming years he drank his way through his fortune and into his coffin.

We have found much satisfaction in these later-life fulfillments of early life desires. By all means, we would say, take the trip, start the business, bake the cake if the urge to do so is strong. Even burn a few late candles if you must, while bearing in mind the hazards of carrying the thing past the point of no return or endangering more vital enterprises.

Here we must distinguish between things anybody can do and things only we older people can do. Only older people can attend to life's crowning achievement, the acquisition of wisdom won by experience and processed by reflection. Whatever else we might do, this, we decided, would have to come first.

As a prerequisite to any wisdom we might eventually acquire, we needed desperately to lay hold of some kind of guiding principle that would stand firm. What was there, in the profusion of scientific, philosophical, and religious ideas which bombarded our minds, that was solid and permanent, common to all and exclusive to none? We found the answer in evolution of consciousness (see Appendixes). This concept became the foundation on which we were to base our preparation.

The idea of evolution has permeated the mind of man from the beginning of recorded human thought. The Hindu Vedas of 2000 B.C. are steeped in it, and it is the keynote of some of the avant-garde movements today's young people are finding so exciting. Religionists find in the evolution of consciousness the very work of God, and it is the sine qua non of creative atheism. Darwin, with his ideas about natural selection and mutation, made evolution the most-discussed scientific topic of the nineteenth century. Julian Huxley illuminated twentieth-century science with his famous 1942 pronouncement that evolution of physical forms had all but ceased. The evolutionary spearhead, he said, had transferred its activity from the physical and unconscious sphere to the realm of conscious mental and social activity. "Evolution," he wrote, "has become conscious of itself." In religious terms, God has given man partnership in his own evolution. What we will ultimately become is now largely up to us.

In Huxley's insight we found a new and cosmic significance to the last third of life. Far from being a meaningless appendage tacked onto the middle years, it is a time provided by nature for the most spectacular advances in the evolution of human consciousness.

Our explorations inwardly have established this point in our minds past any possibility of doubt. As we have examined the general state of human consciousness in the large (see Appendixes) and our own personal psyches in the particular, we have grown more and more aware of the need to free the human spirit from the tribal-nature automatisms that have for so long held it prisoner.

The most casual glance at today's world scene is enough to show that release from such tribalism is mankind's most urgent need. We find Hindu and Muslim, Jew and Arab, Catholic and Protestant, Communist and capitalist continually at each other's throats with dagger and bomb. We find most of mankind's energies tied up in tribe-centered programs of tribal "honor" and intertribal destruction, with these programs exploding every quarter century or so into global conflicts of mounting terror and ferocity. These tribal rivalries have dominated human history for a million years, and no modern country is exempt from them. Unless the antidote is applied they will destroy us.

The antidote is well known: it is wisdom, the philosophical serenity and detachment that most naturally flowers in the last third of life. The world has never stood in more desperate need of wisdom than now.

Man has been on earth for more than two million years. At the time of his first appearance, nature was involved in a great evolutionary experiment to determine what species would eventually dominate the planet. The predators, particularly the big cats and dogs—lions, tigers, hyenas, wolves, coyotes— had a formidable lead. They were well established on an earth already some five billion years old. It seemed unlikely that any new species would overthrow them. They were powerful, fast, well armed, wily, ruthless, and some had mastered teamwork in the hunt.

Yet fangless, clawless, unfurred man turned out to be the most ferocious predator yet evolved. Originating on the jungle fringe, he moved into protected caves and from there quickly fanned out to take command of the plains, the high hills, and the oceans. He did so by developing unparalleled skills in the arts of team hunting. Nothing could stand against him, and quite soon, as geologic time goes, the forests were hunted clean of the great meat herds, the fish in streams, lakes, and oceans were dwindling or gone, and there was nothing left for man to hunt but others of his kind. The hunting horn became the army bugle and the big game became "the enemy"—himself!

This brought man to an evolutionary crisis he has not yet completely solved. As the winning predator, he had emerged to dominate the earth. But clearly, if he continued as pure competitive predator, he would prey on his own kind until his species was self-destroyed. The evolutionary process was confronted with a profound dilemma. Could a predator possibly evolve into something else? None ever had. Man the great predator seemed doomed.

At this point nature produced an evolutionary

miracle, the agriculturist. The hunt, whether for man or beast, now became obsolete; meat and grain could be had by simple nonviolent cooperation with nature. There quickly evolved corollary types, the trader who distributed the new abundance and the scholar and teacher who preserved the peaceful arts that made civilized life possible. For a brief moment of history man's dilemma seemed solved.

But only briefly. Even a force so powerful as the evolutionary drive could not break, overnight, hunting habits of a million years' standing. Come a fright, a fit of temper, or a crop failure and man quickly reverted to his old ways. The hunting horn/army bugle reappeared, tribal "honor" and hunting organization were reinvoked, and man was off once again to the slaughter. It is, of course, suicidal folly. But it is this very self-destruction that immediately threatens the continuance of our species, for the agriculturist has come to hunt the land as destructively as the warrior hunts his own kind. If unchecked, the species is on its way to quick extinction.

And only we elders are situated to do anything about it. People of the early and middle years are too enmeshed in natural and tribal automatisms to be able to think independently about the overall needs of the species. Having just finished living through them, we know these middle-year burdens well. We vividly recall the absorbing decades during which the individual asserts and establishes his place in the tribe, takes up the tribal rituals, hunts and chants, establishes his sexuality, and goes through the rites of passage, courtship, mating, and child-rearing. These are jam-packed years, leaving little time for anything else. Children and tribal position demand food, shelter, clothes, and instruction, and the tribe does not give these things without its price: two or three decades of tribal servitude and conformity. The challenge to those of us who have paid this price and been released is to show that we can evolve from tribal consciousness to global and even cosmic awareness.

The entire significance of the last third of our lives rests on our ability to turn this trick. For the first time in our lives we are free spirits—free of parental and tribal domination, free from unthinking family routines, ritualistic competitiveness, and institutionalized hostility, free to think and act for ourselves, free to open our minds and our lives to new thoughts and fresh experience, free to criticize tribal homilies when we find them vicious or stupid, free to deny the prehistoric-hunter archetype in us and to bring forward the arts and skills of the agriculturist, the philosopher, and even the saint.

The saying that youth is the hope of the world is tribal rubbish. Youth is too enmeshed in the snares of archetypal nature to be the hope of anybody, even of itself. If there is hope for mankind it lies not in the fire of youth but in the wisdom of age. *We* are man's hope. It is we who must give youth its hope and its freedom by ending the tribal trash we now stuff their dear defenseless heads with and by teaching them the glory of cosmic truth—after first learning it ourselves. This is the evolutionary purpose of the last third of life. This is the reason we have been given that magnificent extension of years that is now upon us. This is why we of the Last Third Club consider Condition Three so vital a turning point. This is why, to fulfill the meaning and purpose of our lives, we must now study, learn, extend ourselves in wisdom as we never have before. This is why "we have decided to use our remaining years primarily for this preparation."

FOUR

We assert that the last third of life is given by nature for this high purpose; that it can illuminate all earlier experience in the joyous fulfillment of a rounded life.

In Number Three we decided to prepare. Very well, what do we do first?—and then what, and what after that? In Condition Four we begin the sequence of answers. What do we do first? We make a decisive move toward a mental plateau that will soon become our habitual stance. We consciously try to shift our point of view from the local to the cosmic. Our new strivings will be rooted not in somebody's offhand idea or opinion but in the basic structure of the universe. Only when we have broken through the fence of particulars into the wide world of universals can we begin to see clearly the dimensions of time and eternity into which the last third of life has thrust us.

Regardless of the particular condition we may be concentrating on at any particular moment, Condition One remains with us as a spur and incentive. We are *different* from the general run of people. Our time is limited. Where the average person may waste a good part of his time, we cannot—there is so little of it left and so much to be accomplished.

So we went after our new job with a will. There is, we learned, a law, operative in all living things, which might be called the Principle of Appropriate Times. This law is noted and celebrated throughout the sacred writings of all cultures—"there is a time for all things"; "a time to be born and a time to die"; "when I became a man I put away childish things"; "my time is not yet come." At the level of plant life it is the most apparent of all laws: there cannot be a plant till there's a seed, or a seed till there's a fertilized flower, or a flower till there's a stem, or a stem till there's a root, or a root till there's a soil-borne, rain-watered, sun-warmed seed.

The principle holds throughout the kingdom of the lower animals: all the essential things of life and growth and development can happen only at their appropriate, carefully prepared times. And when such a time comes, what is scheduled to happen *must* happen if the organism is to continue to its next stage of development. The final, highest stage is always found to have a meaning beyond the life cycle of the individual organism—a meaning that is transindividual, transtribal, transspecies, ecological, transcendent. The organism must do, or have done to it, the right thing at the right time or it misses the full realization of its life potential. No stage is accidental, without purpose, or superfluous; the going-to-seed is as important as the sprouting.

When we applied this principle to our own lives it completely overturned our conventional ways of thinking about the human life cycle on earth. In the average urban society of our time, it is assumed that one is born, grows up, enters a period it is conventional to consider "productive," and then begins a kind of death-in-life called "retirement," widely regarded as a period of general decline, a kind of anteroom to death, which is thought to be the end of everything.

The Principle of Appropriate Times revealed the cruel fallacy in this line of thought. There was every reason to think that the more highly developed, more complex, more sensitive human organism would evolve an even more intense significance in its allotted time intervals than the vegetable order of creation.

Comprehension dawned—it was so! We had completed our sprouting and growing phase, had yielded our branches, leaves, and flowers, and now were entering the most important phase of all. Out of our vast experience we were now expected to produce seeds. These were to have a quality and completeness that could not appear at any other time of life; the necessary perspective and experience was lacking until now. These seeds were the most precious of all human creations. They were essential to our personal development and vital to the continuance of our species. They were the seeds of wisdom.

The briefest glance at the condition of mankind on earth today is enough to show the need for this life-giving spiritual vitamin. For lack of wisdom we are making a hell out of what could be a paradise and a misery out of what could be a joy. Our actions contradict and nullify each other. All nations loudly proclaim their love of peace and all bankrupt themselves on preparations for war. We watch with alarm the destruction of land, sea, and air, yet heap on these same life sustainers our ever-increasing loads of poisons, pollutants, and life destroyers. We spend large sums informing each other that excessive use of nicotine or alcohol can produce particularly unpleasant terminal illnesses—and even larger sums promoting the widespread use of these same drugs. Careful and expensive research by some of our best minds has shown that earth cannot sustain our present population increase for more than another century— yet in most of the leading countries (including the United States) the production of children remains at suicidally high levels. We complain about the bitter competition in the manufacture and sale of things we have plenty of (cars, refrigerators, cookies) yet have not turned our hand to increase the supply of things that are in dire scarcity (education, good housing, adequate diet, health care, usable mass transportation). We spend billions on the conscious production of folly (deliberately vapid escape entertainment for television and cinema) and choke off every attempt at the further dissemination of serious knowledge. . . .

The list could go on endlessly. Where is the wisdom? Obviously it is undersupplied. Why? Mostly because we in the last third of life, a time specifically provided by nature for the production of wisdom, have failed to produce it in the required quantity.

The frivolities in which we see our contemporaries squandering these precious years (follies many of us once took part in!) are nothing short of appalling. Everywhere we see the lost people of our older generation in dazed and empty-minded window-shopping; buying with much fuss, study, and bickering trinkets they don't need and nobody particularly wants; traveling, simply to fill the time, to places they have no interest in; pouring precious days, weeks, years into pointless table games; collecting worthless junk or puttering at useless chores and trying to dignify these futilities by the name of "hobbies"; talking endlessly about food and diets and restaurants where they have sampled the fare; pestering grownup offspring with visits, gifts, and phone calls in an effort to keep alive a relationship long since outgrown; running from doctor to doctor and from climate to climate, making a career of their symptoms; doing everything they can, in short, to avoid the one thing the last third of life is given for—the cultivation within themselves of the wisdom their species so desperately needs.

If anyone is to blame it is ourselves. And the blame cannot be social or corporate; it cannot be historical or inherited; it is personal. No one of us *had* to follow so blindly a life-style that would leave us so spiritually and emotionally bankrupt in our later years (or *did* we?). The realities of these last years did not come upon us suddenly, they only seemed to. Actually we had known all our lives that they would come.

Now they are here. Try as we will, we cannot conceal our emotional impoverishment from ourselves. If we were heavily job-oriented, it is not easy to change that orientation; the fact that we are no longer wanted at the office, store, shop, or plant comes hard, no matter how we may strive to put a brave face on it. If we were family-oriented, the fact that the family no longer needs our parental management comes no more easily. Wherever we turn, doors that once were open to us are closing, and we have not yet found the new ones opening. Old routines are drying up, losing their meaning and excitement, and we have not created the new ones that are to take their place. If we try to look and act young we only make ourselves ridiculous, yet we don't as yet know any other way to look and act. We must deal with the sad fact that we have grown old without knowing how to be old.

This is the most dangerous passage of our transition. It has led people into sourness, permanent depression, even suicide. Yet go through it we must; there is no other way to our goal. And we must pass through most of it alone. If our aim is individual enlightenment and growth, our trip must be personal and solitary. The old outgrown patterns must be abandoned—this we know. We know also that this will mean a stretch of suffering and inner desolation. So we take up our burden and begin our journey, sustained only by the hope that we may not be too long in darkness before the first streaks of dawn begin to show and by the sure knowledge that the path to wisdom must of necessity traverse these bleak and forbidding slopes.

The unexamined life, Socrates said, is not worth living, and Wordsworth counseled that the way to understand one's emotions was to recollect them in tranquillity. We had reached a point where these abstract philosophical principles had become, for a time, our daily bread. If we had to choose between pain and futility, we'd take the pain. We set ourselves to review our lives in the blinding new light of our blinding new realities.

At first we seemed beset on all sides with insurmountable contradictions. If our work lives of performing programed tasks had been brought to an end by compulsory retirement, and if the other programs available to us seemed empty and futile, what was the point of effort—*any* effort? If the reason for marriage—the family—was now phased out, what was the point of marital fidelity—or *any* fidelity? The broad way of indolent living and sexual promiscuity opened before us as among our possible choices. But to many of us this was morally distasteful. Even those of us who were less firmly bound by moral considerations found drawbacks in this route. Some of us had already traveled it far enough to learn that it does indeed lead to destruction. But we still had not found the narrow way that was supposed to lead to eternal life. And the lives and characters of the moralists we knew strongly suggested that they hadn't found it either. Our dilemma was extreme. The old programing had failed our biocomputers, and any new program we could conceive of led ultimately to the same blind alley. We were close to despair. As forces capable of directing our lives, our intellects had failed us.

Right here, at the very point of our extremest futility, into the blackest corner of our darkness, came the first ray of light. We remembered something we had heard somewhere, or read somewhere, or that just came spontaneously from our deeper consciousness: intellect was never *supposed* to direct our lives.

Thought was a tool to be used, and intellect was a servant to be assigned set tasks; neither was ever designed to be placed in command of our lives. As one authority, Joseph Pearce, put it, intellect is a horse, meant to pull the cart and not to drive it.

With this enlightenment we experienced another spurt of progress. True, our freedom contained some frightening possibilities. But it also contained some sublime ones. At least we had discovered, finally, what it was we had to do. We had to find that principle within us, other than thought or intellect, that could guide and direct the last third of our lives with perfect competence. We were now on our way to those experiences which would fill and round out our lives.

FIVE

We have resolved to give over our lives to Cosmic Creative Intelligence as we individually name and experience this divine force.

We now approached another pivotal point. If our vaunted brains could no longer be counted on to guide us, what could? If the combination of human energy and human intelligence that had served us so long and carried us so far was inadequate to our new life needs, what could take its place?

For a time, this one had us fumbling in the dark. We'd puzzle over it, reject the whole idea that our own wits couldn't handle all life's problems, reconsider, ponder some more. Finally, simply by asking more questions—and more and more and more—the answers began to come.

Q: Where did these brains we were so proud of come from?

A: They were given us.

Q: By whom?

A: By our genetic heritage.

Q: Come now, you can do better than that. Where did human intelligence come from?

A: From the nature of things. From the universe. The cosmos.

Q: From Cosmic Creative Intelligence?

A: You could put it that way if you wanted to.

Q: Then there is another realm of intelligence than the human?

A: There must be. Otherwise...

Q: Never mind the otherwise; what makes you think so?

A: By seeing what it does. Even the simplest living plant is an intellectual achievement staggeringly beyond anything the human intelligence could manage. And when you consider the human body . . .

Q: All right, what about this Other Intelligence? What is it mainly interested in?

A: I—I can't really say. It always seems to want to create and develop new things.

Q: Would you say, then, that its main concern on earth was evolution?

A: Yes, of course, that's it—evolution.

Q: Your own evolution, possibly?

A: Well, I can't say as to that.

Q: But possibly?

A: Yes, possibly—after all, anything is possible . . .

Q: Now we're getting somewhere. If anything is possible, and if Cosmic Creative Intelligence is interested in evolving things then that Intelligence might be interested in evolving—you?

A: Well, possibly.

Q: Do you consider yourself fully evolved in your present condition?

A: God, no!

Q: There's more to be done on the project called You?

A: A great deal more.

Q: Then if this Higher Intelligence is interested in that kind of project, It might help you?

A: It might.

Q: In other words you might get some help from God?

God! Now the cat was out of the bag. They were trying to fob off that same old . . .

At this point some of us gave vent to feelings—strongly negative feelings—about our experiences with purveyors of religious doctrine and aired resentments that had been festering for a long time. Many of us had been deeply wounded during our most impressionable years by inept, often stupid, and sometimes even vicious tub-thumpers for religion. We had had the sayings of Jesus, Moses, and the prophets hammered into our heads by people who quite obviously were not following these precepts in their own lives. As a result, some of us became so allergic to the word God that the mere mention of it was enough to snap our minds shut and lock them. And now here it was again! Quite a number of us almost quit The Last Third Club then and there. It was only the bleak alternatives left us by our sterile Age of Heroic Materialism that kept us searching.

Out of consideration for our own sensibilities in this regard, we decided, when the time came to formulate our experiences for those who had never heard of us, to use the term Cosmic Creative Intelligence when referring to the supreme creating principle of the universe.

This, however, does not mask the fact that we are talking about the same Power to whom a lot of people give the name God. We have, in fact, no intention of masking this fact. We want to reach as many people in the last third of life as we can—those whose early religious experiences were pleasant and those who have known some unpleasantness. Many of the "God" people," we soon discovered, are just as indignant over the horrors committed in the name of religion as the "Cosmic Creative Intelligence" people. But for the special conditions that prevail on entering Condition Five we have other reasons for using the term Cosmic Creative Intelligence.

What we are interested in is not the various names given to reality, but Reality itself. And the most emphatic reality in the visible, steadily experienced, physical universe is the existence and constant operation of a Cosmic Creative Intelligence that is continually active whether our various individual intelligences are aware of it or not. The question is, do we want to cooperate with it in the overall evolutionary enterprise? This is not a group question but a personal one. Since evolution began before we were born and will continue after we die, it's a question that transcends even birth and death. It involves no one but Cosmic Creative Intelligence and personal individual intelligence. It's a simple yes or no: Do you want to cooperate or not?

No one could decide it for us but ourselves, functioning as solitary individuals—though in making so important a decision we thought it prudent to summon all the help, in the form of relevant background information, that we could lay our hands on.

The "call him God" people among us protested that Cosmic Creative Intelligence is a misnomer, since the Power responsible for the creation of the universe possesses a great many qualities besides intelligence. We agree entirely and will confront some of these other qualities later on. In Condition Five, however, we are addressing ourselves exclusively to the factor of intelligence—and for good reason. The human intellect, particularly in our floundering Age of Heroic Materialism, is excessively clamorous and demanding. Intoxicated by its extraordinary success in limited areas, it makes exaggerated claims for itself. It gives us no peace to reflect in other dimensions until its demands are dealt with. For now, therefore, we narrow down to the direct confrontation of personal and Cosmic Intelligence.

There is no question as to which is the greater and which the lesser, which the original and which derivative, which the trunk and which the branch. Our immediate concern was the *attitude* of the greater toward the lesser—is it friendly, hostile, or just indifferent? The answer, as far as our personal lives were concerned, became more and more clear. Some power outside ourselves had not only provided the means of our creation but also the means of our survival for five or six decades or more through the multiple dangers of life on a precarious planet. We remembered our numerous close calls, incredible recoveries, preposterous windfalls, and unmerited blessing and accepted this as evidence, in our own lives at least, of a cosmic benevolence.

But still the restless human intellect was unsatisfied. "So you have been lucky," it told us. "What about those who have not?" We were obliged to face up to the unaccountable malevolence that exists on earth alongside incredible goodness. How does one answer that? This drove us into speculations far beyond the usual ruts of our workaday minds. We had to return to the question of what Cosmic Creative Intelligence is mainly interested in. Surely it wasn't justice in any human sense. Then which was at fault, the cosmic sense of justice or the human? But the human sense of justice, we observed, could not be accurately defined, since it was in a constant process of evolution. It was a long span from the ancient and still extant eye-for-an-eye and tooth-for-a-tooth to the modern avantgarde jurisprudence which views crime as an illness to be healed rather than a crime to be punished. Was it possible that an advanced concept of justice might govern one sphere of human life, while primitive vengeance, or even the cruel indifference of primordial nature, might prevail in others? We found no pat answer.

Perhaps Cosmic Creative Intelligence was not primarily interested in "justice" as human intelligence conceives it. If that's the case, what is it interested in that the human mind *can* conceive? That was much easier for us. Both the living and the fossil records gave clear evidence of the cosmic intent. It was to create freedom—measureless, unbounded, physical, intellectual, emotional, and spiritual freedom.

The visible work on earth began, of course, with the physical. The original life-forms of earth had very little freedom. The plants were rooted to the ground. Even their progeny had no freedom of movement except at seed time, when their location was determined by chance eddies of air and water. The amoeba, a fairly advanced creature as primitive life-forms go, could reproduce only by dividing itself in two, could exist only in moisture, could move only by continually changing its semifluid shape.

The gill-breathing vertebrate fish greatly advanced the cause of freedom. He could utilize the extra strength packed into the big protein molecules built by the lower life-forms. He could range the sea and even experience, in momentary leaps, that strange new medium above him, the air. The creative impulse soon mastered that too, and at length produced that masterpiece of physical freedom, the duck, who could freely make his way in water, land, and air.

We need not trace the creative steps to man, except to point out that it was an unbroken sequence to a creature who, in the physical realm, can cruise under the sea, voyage on the surface of the oceans, journey at high speed on the land, range through the atmosphere to great altitudes, and even cruise in outer space to neighboring celestial bodies—and, in nonphysical space, range the whole kingdom of the human creative imagination and even experience, in momentary leaps of altered states of consciousness, the transcendental. More than that, man can actually control given physical substance to the extent of giving material form to many of his intangible imaginings. Here is freedom in breathtaking abundance! Here is unequivocal expression of the divine creative intent.

But the impulse to freedom makes it clear to the

heart of man that its work has only begun. No man or woman feels himself free. Even if he may have won wide physical freedoms, he is fettered by mental chains that often seem as strong as iron ones. The man who believes he must not go through an open door is as securely jailed as if he were locked in a maximum-security prison. Mental blocks, institutionalized fears, custom, rigid ideas imprinted early and long conditioned into ruts, fixed notions, tribal taboos, and expectations, all hold him back from the full realization of the exalted spiritual freedoms Cosmic Creative Intelligence clearly has in mind for him.

This last may seem a bold statement. How can we presume to speak for the infinite cosmic mind, out of our local and finite minds, to the extent of saying what it "clearly has in mind"? Partly by what Kierkegaard called the "leap of faith," partly by the message of our own hearts' deep longing for a new and special kind of freedom.

We had by this time learned that at the core of our being lived a body-generating Self, with capabilities of which we had not dreamed and with yet unsuspected possibilities such as to fire our imagination to dare new peaks. We had learned that the stretch of human earth life we were now traversing—the last third—was given for the express purpose of breaking out of our tribal mental fetters into new coordinates of Self-realization. We had come to see that the relation between ourselves and Cosmic Creative Intelligence was, among other things, an intellectual one: we were expected to use our heads.

It was the relation of an infinite cosmic mind to a limited local mind. Communication between the two might be compared to a broadcasting enterprise with listener feedback. The receiving is meditation; the feedback is prayer. The individual receiving set can be heard only within a narrow local circle and can receive only that part of the total broadcast band that its tuning equipment permits. But here the broadcast analogy breaks down. Radio receiving sets cannot increase their built-in capacity to receive, or decide to give themselves over to a single station. Human beings can.

Our discovery that this is so establishes us in Condition Five and prepares us for Condition Six. We now have achieved a new open-mindedness toward metaphysical reality. We can begin—some of us for the first time in our lives—to take more seriously some of the things the great cosmos-oriented minds of all ages, including our own, have been trying to get across to us.

SIX

Through regular morning and evening meditations we are finding ourselves more and more in harmony with this transcendent Power.

"It seems to me," wrote Henry David Thoreau after a sequence of experiences in deep meditation, "that we may safely *trust* a great deal more than we do." [1] Thoreau was speaking out of a long tradition. Meditation has been the practice of seekers after wisdom for at least ten thousand years, and it is being widely rediscovered in our own time. Its essence, as the American sage implied, is a deep and abiding *trust* in the moving spirit of the universe—in God.

In Condition Six we are ready for our first bold venture into the metaphysical unknown. In Condition Five we identified intellect as a problem-solving tool, indispensable to functioning in the field of action, adept at finding solutions to equations stated in the known quantities of here and now. In Condition Six we pass beyond the reach of intellect, leaving it behind while, in trust, we allow ourselves to be taken into the care of the Infinite.

It is not, however, a blind trust, nor have the prudent questions of intellect been ignored. In fact, the reassuring answers to these questions bring us to the springboard from which we may confidently take our leap of faith. It is a leap from workaday fact into a mysterious but potent Beyond, from the sphere of action to the realm of Being. It is taken in the firm belief that in this direction can be found much of the earthly wisdom we and the world need here and now, as well as the celestial insights that are such valuable preparation for the hour of our transition.

This sounds like a large order, and it is—but by now we were ready for it. We had faced the fact that our days of biological existence on this planet were numbered and that their number was not large. We realized we could easily diddle away the rest of our lives in fruitless debate over the pros and cons of our future. It was time to quit fooling around. We made our decision. It was in favor of a continuing life in another realm of consciousness. We decided to make our first tentative explorations of these territories.

Scientists, using the electroencephalograph to chart brain waves, have identified four levels of consciousness—waking state, deep sleep, dreaming sleep, and Fourth State. It is this mysterious Fourth State of Consciousness that we enter when we meditate.

The benefits of meditation have been known since the very earliest times, though exactly what happens during the process remains a (so far) unfathomed mystery. Those knowledgeable in harmonics (see Appendix) point out that everything in creation is in harmonic relationship with everything else and hint that meditation may bring the Self into conscious harmony with the divine, radiant Source. Whether this or something else happens, all who have participated in the practice agree that it is beneficial, and behavioral scientists have reported that it can reduce elevated blood pressure, increase intellectual performance, and enhance the general sense of well-being.

However this may be, it is important to successful meditation that one not anticipate anything but deep silence. If something extraordinary is found in the silence well and good, but it should not be put there by wishful imagining. So many tales of visions, ecstasies, and transports have been spread as to make this warning necessary. One must let come what will come.

Trying to force the result into a preconceived form, we found, only results in fantasy and mood-making. It tends to nullify the meditation and reduce its benefits. The whole approach should be effortless and strainless. The key phrase for Condition Six is "Easy does it," and the easier the better.

What one "does" in meditation is simple enough; it amounts almost to "not doing." "I loafe and invite my soul," [2] wrote Walt Whitman, who was one of the most successful of all American meditators. Certainly the spirit of loafing, in the sense of detaching oneself from everyday concerns and declaring a mental vacation, is one of the essentials.

Some of us have found it helpful to give over a whole day or two, now and then, to just being quiet. One must pick his time, though, and be in the mood. A good time is after a period when one has had a lot to do with people and is ready for a little solitude (we try to keep our lives in balance; sometimes the difficulty is not too much involvement but too much of being by ourselves). At such times, though it may sound strange at first, this complete break from people, this getting by oneself and trying to know the quiet, is to many of us the essential point of meditation, high in dividends.

If one wants to make a project of it, one may get up when it's still dark on a chosen day and watch for the dawn—the new beginning. The way dawn comes is always a special and fine excitement, too often missed. Things seem to know it's coming; the quiet of the night seems to deepen a little just before first light. Then the light changes and the predawn twilight is there, a filtered presence. One may think of the great arc of light advancing over the earth and of all the creatures greeting it: a forest full of birds in song, a rooster crowing somewhere. Presently the sun breaks the horizon, rapidly clears the earth, and begins its climb.

All day one may keep track of the sun. If one can manage it, a walk on a wooded road or in a park, or along a river or lake or the sea, may prove a good thing, or a drive to a distant place, planning to have lunch where nobody knows one. One may have cleared the project with one's family—who must come to understand that apartness is as much a part of family life as togetherness—and have arranged that business demands be not pressing; then one can give oneself to the day. Noon comes. At sea the navigators are watching through their sextants; they check their chronometers and know where they are.

Sunset, twilight, dark, the moon and stars—one begins to know a little of where one is too. All day one has not thought of people, but of earth and sun, daylight and dark. When thoughts of people intrude, one chooses the people of whom one will think, choosing solitary, day-conscious people—the psalmist lifting his eyes to the hills whence cometh his strength, the young prophet walking in the desert and encountering his destiny, the Lake Poet considering the English countryside, the physicist perceiving that space is curved. All are people who have made the meditator's big discovery—that man's earthly poise is related to his awareness of time and place, earth and sun. Sometimes there comes a great moment of full knowledge of being an earth creature and belonging, wholly content. This delicious instant is frequently reported. It may be described as a sudden intuition that the whole of creation is offered for one, that one is part of a mighty cosmic creative current, forever secure. One is not always so fortunate as to know this moment on the day one has chosen. But a moment comes when one knows it's time for the return to people and the hurly-burly and to see, refreshed, what contribution one can make.

But meditation is more than just being physically quiet (though it *has* been said that prayer is telling God something and meditation is listening to his reply). And, of course, in the busy world so many of us know even in "retirement," one feels limited in the number of days he can take to loaf and invite his soul. One must hit on something one can do every day, regardless of circumstance. The authorities we consulted assured us that fifteen minutes in the early morning and another quarter hour in the late afternoon would be quite long enough, especially in the beginning, and surely anyone can spare that much time for a project of penultimate importance.

"Meditate" . . . what did it mean? The authorities seemed to agree that, whatever else it meant, you had to be alone, by yourself, and you had to be quiet. Really alone. And really quiet. Quiet not just in the ears, but deep in the body, deep in the mind, a very deep, still, soul quiet. Muddy water, runs an old Chinese proverb, if allowed to be still, becomes clear water—as the muddied mind allowed to be still becomes clear. The turmoil simmers down, if one can wait a bit, put aside distractions with sufficient firmness, really want to be quiet and listen. To many of us, meditation need be no more than that—being quiet and listening to the inward silence, fifteen minutes in the morning, another quarter hour in late afternoon.

Others of us have found one or another of the various formal meditative techniques to be helpful. What we are seeking, of course, is the Self, the true Self that resides in each of us and knows its—and our—true relationship to the cosmos. We discovered that there are as many adaptations of the basic techniques for reaching the Self as there are human beings.

Sometimes Self is reached with no techniques at all —spontaneously. But both Self and intellect must be willing, and so some mental preparation seems advisable. Self, we have been assured, is by its essential nature always willing. Since intellect cannot know this until it has experienced it, intellect must make appropriate adjustments. The best attitude for those burdened with reservations is, it seems to us, the experimental one—"we will try it and see."

Since, according to ancient tradition and modern experience, Self is "separate from action," the meditator must, if he is to achieve Self-realization, erase from consciousness all action or memory of action or plans for action, and all sense impressions, during the period of his meditation. To encounter Being he must temporarily move entirely out of the domain of stimulus and response—transcend it— and see what realms may lie beyond.

As final preparation he calls to mind his basic cosmic situation. He is a consciousness resident in a body being carried with four billion others of his kind on a space-floating ball, along with uncountable swarms of other life-forms. He then turns his attention intimately to his earth-dwelling equipment. He becomes aware of his breathing: the downward motion of his diaphragm on inhaling, the upward movement on exhaling. Then, taking a deep breath or two for each station, he lets himself be aware of five stations of consciousness, moving upward along his spinal column: the sensory center for sexual reproduction; the feeling centers of nourishment-digestion-elimination; the solar-plexus seat of jungle alertness and animal self-preservation; the heart-respiration-thorax area where reside the life breath, the heartbeat, and the feeling centers of courage and compassion; and the cranial area which serves as local clearinghouse of the higher consciousness. Presently the feelings from all these centers may converge in a rippling upward flow, centering in the "single eye" of the forebrain, in the forehead between the eyes. Mind may now reciprocate by sending waves of relaxation downward, flooding the body with a glowing sense of peace and ease. This same result is gained by some meditators by simply sitting quietly for a minute or two. Mind and body are now ready to begin meditation. This will be without strain or effort, a natural thing that needs no forcing. The meditator is simply permitting the evolutionary element in him to find and express itself; all he has to do is cooperate with evo-nature, the highest echelon of nature. Mind *wants* to find Self— it is mind's supreme joy—and will do so if allowed to find its own way.

There are several ways, known since antiquity and checked out in recent experience, of keeping the mind thought-free and thus open to awareness of Being, or Self. One is the mandala method, in which the meditator visualizes a square design and concentrates on the changes at its center. Another is the color method, in which the meditator sees in his mind's eye a sequence of colors from infrared through red, orange, yellow, green and blue to violet and ultra-violet, ending in pure white light. Another is the blackboard method, in which the meditator makes his mind a blackboard and erases thoughts from it as fast as they appear. And finally there is the mantra method. The theory of the mantra is as follows:

We know from experience that the life of the mind is a continuous sequence of separate thoughts, one following another in unending flow. All these thoughts are regarded as emanating from Self—the very center we seek to reach. In theory, then, if we could follow any one of these thoughts to its source we would arrive at Self. But problems arise from the fact that all these thoughts filter through a highly stressed central nervous system, where they become freighted with imprinted and conditioned action patterns, diverting mind from its immediate purpose of Self-realization. A roadblock—what to do? Ages ago mind came up with its own solution: the mantra. A mantra is simply a meaningless word whose sound is agreeable, when pronounced with the inner voice to the inner ear, to the mind. The mantra is a thought; it is injected into the ceaseless thought sequence until it finally excludes all other thoughts and takes it over. Since the mantra has no meaning and hence suggests no action it clears a straight channel to Self; when the goal is reached the mantra disappears, leaving mind and Self in joyous union. Theoretically, almost any imagined verbal sound can serve as a mantra. In some religions, prayer chains, providing they have become so mechanical as to have lost their conscious meaning content, have been found to have a mantric effect. If one takes formal instruction in meditation, one's teacher usually assigns a mantra he thinks appropriate. Many thousands of meditators use the mystic word "om," silently repeated with a rhythm suitable to the meditator. Repeating his mantra, he lets his mind sink deeper and deeper inwardly, toward the origin of his repeated mantra sound, toward the center of his being, toward Self.

Along the way, thoughts, feelings, ideas may intrude, sometimes with a seeming urgency, sometimes with remembered pain, pleasure, or rage. These thoughts are not thrust aside and no effort is made to repress them. They are treated as scenery might be by a passenger on his way to a set destination. They are tolerated until they pass, but they are not allowed to stop the journey—the return to the mental repetition of the mantra, which, in a succession of purposeful dives into the upwelling thought flow toward its deep source, continues to carry the mind toward the Self. It may not arrive at its destination at every sitting, but it is not necessary for successful meditation that it should. All that is necessary during the beginning years is the fifteen minutes every morning and another fifteen minutes every afternoon, without judgment as to whether any single meditation is "successful." In the psychology of Self, all meditation is regarded as successful, since it carries one closer to one's radiant, creative core. All religious faiths have their own traditions of meditation (the Quakers have a particularly effective one). Having found that individual meditators make their individual adjustments to whatever tradition they adopt, we espouse no particular method. All methods have in common the great essentials—detachment from everyday affairs, abandonment of all desire, cessation of conscious thought, concentration toward that core of oneself that sways to the great universal rhythms of Cosmic Creative Intelligence, the Source Itself—God.

Sometimes, we have found, one may be overtaken by feelings that his meditations are getting nowhere, that the whole business is an empty charade. These spells, we are convinced, are nothing but temptations to spiritual sloth. We advise doggedly "meditating through" them on regular twice-daily quarter hours, come what may. Eventually the light that cannot be extinguished shines for us again, and we are stronger for our ordeal. A little fable comes to us from India, illustrating the point. Two frogs were hopping gaily along one day when they inadvertently hopped into an open milk can half full of milk. They kicked and swam frantically, but the sides of the can were steep and smooth and they could not hop out. After many frustrating circles, one frog announced his intention to give up. He stopped kicking, sank to the bottom, and drowned. "No," resolved the other frog, "I'll keep kicking as long as there's a single kick left in me."

He kicked and kicked and finally, on the point of exhaustion, gave what he was sure must be his one last kick—and found himself vaulting over the edge of the can into the open air, sunshine, and freedom. His long kicking had churned a substantial lump of butter, which gave his last powerful kick the purchase it needed to lift him free.

In a little time, our twice-daily meditations become the spiritual dynamo that powers our drive toward higher consciousness and greater wisdom. Perhaps our meditation provides only a brief instant when the spark passes—that spark of joy and serenity that words cannot describe—but it is enough to transform our whole day. The difference between the day with that spark and the day without it is infinite. It is thus that we are finding ourselves, day by day, more and more in harmony with the transcendent Power.

SEVEN

Reviewing our past in the company of other Last Thirders has shown us that our earlier life goals no longer suffice.

"This world is a bridge," runs an old Chinese proverb; "cross it, but build no house upon it." In Condition Seven the force of this adage has begun, slowly and sometimes painfully, to impress itself upon us. Our regular meditations have brought us more and more under the conscious influence of Cosmic Creative Intelligence. That which is cosmic cannot be exclusively local, individual, clannish, or tribal. Though inclusive of all these subdivisions of consciousness, it transcends them in its own all-pervading light.

As this light grows stronger within us, the confrontation with our ingrained localisms becomes more and more stressful. Our deep minds, in meditation, have recognized Cosmic Creative Intelligence as the prime source of all joy, all creativity, all love, and all harmony and have freely and gladly chosen it above all other alternatives.

But as Jesus of Nazareth reminded us, no man (or woman) can serve two masters. We are still living in a bone-and-muscle society of immature predatory carnivores. Our central nervous systems are heavily imprinted with decades of conditioning to its shibboleths and tribalisms. These habits of thought cannot be cast off all at once; indeed, we have to keep some of them operational as a simple matter of survival. Yet one by one they are being seen through. Their inherent inadequacies become more and more obvious, and we cannot in good conscience cling to them exclusively. Some of our most cherished loyalties are thus demolished, leaving us nothing, for the time being, but the sad wreckage of an outgrown value system. The experience can be desolating. What to do? Where to turn?

We have now arrived at the reason why we call ourselves a club. *We are not going it alone.* We have ample and warmhearted company to carry us over the bleak stretches. Many of these men and women are going over the same bumps we are. Some have already passed over them and emerged radiant and confident, to become inspirations to the rest of us. We share our experiences; all contribute to that pooled reservoir of strength we call the club.

A club is a social thing, and there is a strong element of the sociable in our joint efforts to raise our level of consciousness and address ourselves to wisdom. We have regular meetings at which we share our experiences, and from our shared experience we learn.

Among the things we have learned are these: Many of the rules we have been given to believe are absolutes have turned out, in the clear light of the higher levels of awareness, to be only relative. And some of the assertions handed us as fact have turned out to be untrue. This is what Dr. Jung meant when he said that the values of the first half of life are not valid for the second. We evaluate according to our level of consciousness, and this, if we have healthy minds, is always expanding. Some time not too long after mid-life, the whole inventory has to be retaken, the shelves restocked, and the shop opened in a new location for a new clientele. During this operation, much of the merchandise left over from the old establishment has to be thrown out.

We began our reassessment by inquiring where we got our original stock in the first place. Where did the ideas come from by which we lived the first half of our lives? They came, of course, from our families, from our parents and parent surrogates. To our surprise we learned, by really looking at the situation, that many of these ideas were irrelevant or dead. Even our parents or parent substitutes had themselves given them up, either to expand into finer, more exciting concepts (in which case they aroused our admiration) or crabbedly to shrink into narrower ones (and disappoint us). Whether in their generation or in our own, it is not so much that the ideas of the first half of life are *wrong* as that they do not *suffice* for the second half. They are not enough. The vague discontents of our later years forced us to take a hard look at the ideas on which had been based our major judgments of right and wrong, good and bad, fair or foul, who's nice and who's not, what's worthwhile and what doesn't matter very much.

In almost every important instance, we found, our basic ideas were family oriented. They had no purpose other than to strengthen the family, reinforce its pre-stressed ideas, enhance its prestige. We were taught to obey those in authority, because those in authority knew better than we did and therefore were invariably right. Sexuality was presented to most of us as something highly suspect if not actually wicked or, which was much worse, unhealthful if not firmly held in line by family and tribal rules. Regardless of intra-mural squabbles, a front of undeviating loyalty to the family banner had to be shown outsiders. Parental pronouncements on politics, religion, ethics, and character (some of which were downright fatuous) had the force of law and philosophy in our lives and were accepted without question.

When we left the family to strike out on our own, we carried so many of the family and tribal precepts with us that in one sense we were not striking out on our own at all but merely carrying into a new milieu our own interpretation of the same clan laws that had governed our childhood, with a slight switching of roles to accommodate the fact that *the* family had now become *our* family.

Youth, except in very rare instances, cannot innovate. What the mass of youth most desires is to win a status-bearing place for itself in the adult tribe—to become a parental figure in a family unit and achieve recognized status in the tribal community. There is much struggle to establish sexual prowess, then offer public proof of it in the form of children, then clinch the matter by bringing home the bacon of economic support. The honors-and-rewards systems of the tribe and nation encourage these ends and discourage others.

Thus the first half of life was mainly taken up with routine, unimaginative, soul-limiting, achievement-and-prestige struggles. There was little strength left over to acquire wisdom, to innovate, or to help alter, in the direction of evolutionary advance, a general status quo that, for all we knew, might have been very much in need of altering. The demands of elemental nature functioning at its basic survival level bled dry our creative resources.

This realization brought to light the further fact that our ideas about "nature" had always been a little lopsided. To the average person (and few of us had pretensions to being much more than average) the term nature was taken to mean the basic reproduction-and-survival mechanisms of humankind operating in an environment of the lower orders of life—plants and animals, birds and fish, trees, insects, and flowers. We learned only belatedly that nature also has a forward thrust, an evolutionary prong. This component carries a drive toward enlightenment, a thirst for wisdom, and an impulse to the highest spiritual aspiration. This evolutionary fountain is just as "natural" as the sex drive (there is, indeed, a school of yoga that claims they spring from the same source, and there are western psychiatrists who agree). Therefore, it is not surprising that we can feel it more sharply in the later years, when the fever of the reproductive phase has been lived out, when the path to creativity is clear and the impulse strong.

Many of us were slow in discovering this path. We teetered on the verge of becoming one of those odious picture-carrying oldsters forever drooling over their grandchildren and thus seeking a vicarious reentry into a reproductive cycle that, in them, nature has finished with—or trying to recapture the excitement of the breadwinning days by "taking an occasional flier." In some of us this kind of dawdling went on for years. The deceptive thing about it was that there did not seem to be anything drastically *wrong* with it, nor was it *entirely* devoid of satisfaction. It was simply that it *did not suffice*—was not enough—did not entirely satisfy. It was rather like a child of high-school age still sucking his thumb. We were somehow not acting our age and were vaguely uneasy about it.

In Condition Seven our meditative contact with Cosmic Creative Intelligence greatly reinforced our natural evolutionary drives, and we began to see in larger dimensions. The view from this dimension overturned a great many of our old beliefs.

There was, for example, the matter of nationhood. Once even a little cosmic perspective is attained, a global view of the world becomes automatic. The sun is known as one of an uncountable swarm of stars called a galaxy, and the earth is one of its planets—a very limited space, a tiny ball. "Our country"—a concept that once seemed vast and all-embracing—shrinks to one of many countries spotting this small earth. All of them are persuaded, just as we are, of the unique excellence of their own nationhood, and all of them are ready to fight to the death at the slightest hint of intrusion by any of the others. The prime current examples of dangerous national tribalisms stem from the worldwide capitalist-Communist confrontation. Each regards the other as greedy, insatiable, and lethal; each has frantically poured its energies into an arms race that has stockpiled the means to destroy the world and everything in it many times over. Cosmically, of course, this is madness. From the cosmic stance it is clear that on our small and crowded globe both systems must survive or neither will; that rampant local nationalisms must give way to global humanitarianism as a simple matter of survival. This undermined one of our proudest boasts and forced us to give up something we had been miscalling our "patriotism." We had to learn how to be loyal to our country through being loyal to our species. For some of us, this was one of the more agonizing of our growing pains.

The institution of marriage also came under review. Many of the men and women who make up The Last Third Club had put an enormous emotional investment into this tribal arrangement over a great many years, only to find that it had lost much of its original meaning in the last third of life. Some of us had reached the stage of those aging couples, so often seen in the more expensive restaurants, who eat but don't speak, having long ago run out of things—even cutting things!—to say to each other and settled into a dead and sterile ennui.

The marriage "made in heaven for all eternity" crumbles under the impact of cosmic awareness. Jesus, among many others, specifically repudiated the

68

"eternal" marriage, explaining that in the kingdom of God no one is married or given in marriage but all are as free spirits. The "made for eternity" notion was manufactured out of politico-economic expediency by the ancient tribal fathers. It is carried into the present because it is considered good for the economy (the tribe) to have men and women firmly tied to each other for as long as possible, and especially during the reproductive and child-rearing years. This perfectly suits the predisposition of those years of fascinated working, playing, and watching together as nature duplicates our bodies in miniature with enchanting variations. It also perfectly suits the needs of our small children, who must have stability and devotion during their formative years.

But when the children are grown, departed, and raising children of their own, the marriage is thrown into crisis. Either it degenerates into a stalemate empty of mutual meaning and interest, or it is re-energized and reborn as both partners discover the evolutionary potential of the last third of their lives, or it is dissolved in separation, divorce, or a quiet going of separate ways. In any event the earlier marriage goals "no longer suffice." The inner drive of the reproductive years is primarily physical and biological; of the later years it is preponderantly spiritual and intellectual. We know of no marriages that have entirely escaped some such crisis in the later years.

The corporation life that dominates so large a part of modern living also thrusts itself forward for re-examination. To many of us, the corporation was for many years the vehicle of status, achievement, success, security, and prestige. Far into the second half of our lives it was a central, if not *the* central, reality. But what had been central became peripheral as cosmic awareness grew. "The company," once it lost its position in the vortex of our lives, began to be seen as one of a great many companies, all of them together taking the form of a great clanking caterpillar tractor crawling across the face of the earth. Calling itself Industrialization, it chews, chops, and gouges natural resources at one end while leaving a trail of profits and poisons at the other. From the point of view of cosmic awareness it is a deadly threat to that thin, life-sustaining ecological film on which all present and future earth life depends. The machine has no driver and no brakes; its appetite grows crazily as we all jump aboard it and force it into more and more scooping and gouging each year in the dubious cause of increasing the GNP. Again we are thrown into painful conflict. Again a life goal which seemed perfectly adequate during the first half of life is seen, during the second half, to have serious limitations.

Similar fates overtook a long series of aims left over from earlier phases. It once appeared to be a prime and worthy goal to have a large family. Now we learned on solid cosmic and global authority that family size must diminish, that the every-quarter-century doubling of population must halt, or all will perish within the next century. Even those most solid of all life's rules—that work is a virtue and that the really good person works continuously, conscientiously, and hard—no longer held; from the cosmic point of view we'd all be better off if some kinds of work were never begun. Creative loafing made more and more sense; we found ourselves leaning more sympathetically toward the Walt Whitman who wrote "I loafe and invite my soul" (an insight that came to him, incidentally, only at the start of the second half of his life). Thus did we truly arrive at Condition Seven, wherein, by reviewing our past in the company of other Last Thirders, we discovered that our earlier life goals no longer suffice.

What we needed, of course, was another set of goals —goals that *would* suffice for the rest of our span on earth, carry us through the transition, and still have some momentum to launch us into the world we enter after abandoning our physical bodies. We had three immediate requirements: wisdom for our remaining earth life, love of the cosmic life-in-God in his joyous creativity, and patience for living the difficult cosmic-local double life of the interim. The search for a fulfillment of these three needs carried us to the threshold of Condition Eight.

EIGHT

Through reading, discussion, and reflection we have humbly attempted to discover and cultivate those higher values that are essential to our new life.

C. G. Jung wrote:

The decisive question for man is: Is he related to something infinite or not? That is the telling question of his life. Only if we know that the thing which truly matters is the infinite can we avoid fixing our interest upon futilities, and upon all kinds of goals which are not of real importance. . . . The more a man lays stress on false possessions, and the less sensitivity he has for what is essential, the less satisfying is his life. . . . If we understand and feel that here in this life we already have a link with the infinite, desires and attitudes change. In the final analysis, we count for something only because of the essential we embody, and if we do not embody that, life is wasted.[1]

In Condition One we owned up to the fact that there is no great immediate future for us here on the earth. During the succeeding steps we become more and more aware of the enormous body of human thought and experience of an infinitely continuing life beyond "death"—an experience of Jung's infinite. In Condition Seven we passed through a crisis of belief. We could go along with the "death-ends-it-all" nihilism so preponderant in our materialistic age, and drag ourselves on toward "the end" in ever-deepening despair, or we could cast our lot with those who chose to believe in a continuing evolution of spirit.

Those who chose the former path dropped out of The Last Third Club and went their way. The rest of us found ourselves with a struggle on our hands.

Belief needs something to feed on. There were forces, sometimes elevating and inspiring, sometimes baffling, sinister, frustrating, that pulled us this way and that. There were times when we felt that, instead of progressing toward a bright and redeeming goal, our efforts were only sinking us deeper into a bog. What we desperately needed was a platform of firm conviction that would give us lasting support. So, using whatever stout planks came ready to hand, we built one. Simply by much trial, many errors, and slow learning from our mistakes, we arrived at certain axioms.

The first of these was a paradox. Though we had to strive continually if our goal was spiritual growth, we also had to accept the fact that our own strivings alone would never carry us to that goal. Here was our situation: After half a century or so of butting heads with our fellow human predatory carnivores we had developed hard-set patterns of suspicion and defense. "Be on your guard" was our habit; you never know whom to trust. Many of us were brought up in such constant fear of parents, parent surrogates, and official authority that our lives consisted almost altogether in placating them and conforming to their edicts. We were taught to hold on to an advantage once you have it; give an inch and you risk losing all. The historic events of our lifetime seemed to provide further basis for fear and suspicion: never in history had there been such widespread and wanton hatred, violence, and destruction so flimsily excused.

Now, near the end of the march, we have more or less dropped out of the parade. Now we spend more time just watching it go by. But our attention is not wholly on the human parade any more; we have begun to notice some other things. We have awakened to the cosmos from which man emerged—the "infinite." We have noticed that it moves not at all with the jerky, frenzied rhythms of machine-age man. As we observe it in the night sky it has a patient majesty of movement, a divine certainty of purpose, and an all-embracing benevolence of intent. As we see it in a snowstorm, where uncountable hexagonal flakes fall with no two exactly alike, we find an inexhaustible creative inventiveness. Where the ecology has not been disrupted by man, we find a gracious balance and a harmonious accommodation of all created things, all accomplished with startling beauty. And finally, through meditation, we have learned that this "infinite" has (in the phrase of C. S. Lewis) "paid us the intolerable compliment" of wanting us to be in harmony with it—to form a working partnership with Cosmic Creative Intelligence. The seemingly sudden switch is almost more than our crabbed, suspicious, earthbound natures can bear. And yet—

And yet, now that we are at last awake to it, we recognize that there has been something of the infinite in and around us all along. The mere fact of our physical survival is empirical proof that the sum of the forces acting on us has been more benevolent than hostile. If we feared our parents' anger, we were sustained by their devotion. If some authorities seemed harsh, others faithfully carried us through the tight spots. The same boundless creativity and benevolence we sensed in infinity had been steadily at work in our own lives; the more consistently we held this truth in mind, the stronger grew our urge toward harmony and union.

Yet we are only earth creatures, rank with the poisons of the factory and heavy with the lusts of the predator. Hence our continuing predicament: however great may be our *desire* for union with Cosmic Creative Intelligence, what are our *means* for this union?

It was in this extremity that we discovered the paradox: You try as hard as you can; your trying won't get you there but you can't get there without it. The last essential bit cannot be taken by force but must be given by grace. Our sustaining faith is that it will be given when the jarring and unharmonious discords have been purged away from us so we can ring true to the cosmic tone. It is rather like trying to hear the striking of a distant clock while in a noisy room. When the hubbub is stilled, the chimes come clear.

What goal, then, might we consciously strive for? The answer—"simple friendliness"—is shockingly naïve, yet it was found only after the most preposterous difficulties. Some of us, afire with enthusiasm to to take the kingdom of heaven by storm and perfect ourselves spiritually *all at once*, did some pretty foolish things. One of our members decided that, after much reading, thought, and meditation, he was operating at such an exalted spiritual level he no longer needed a watch but could depend on his new sense of cosmic time to keep him unfailingly on schedule. After a sorry sequence of botched meetings, missed trains, delayed appointments, and business chaos he came back, a sadder but wiser seeker, to telling time the way the rest of us do.

Sometimes, in sheer excess of enthusiasm, we try to "capture God" by intense effort. This path, we find, does not always produce results as certainly as the route of simple friendliness. This seems to be the highest state attainable by our own efforts. Apparently, feeling a deep peace with other human beings induces the harmony with the universe we might otherwise seek in vain. When we drop our fear of others' anger and acknowledge them as selves like our own self and part of the divine Self, when we freely forgive whatever there is to be forgiven, the object of our heart's desire begins to emerge. "The aura of the mystics and the halo of the saints," writes John White in his *The Highest State of Consciousness*, "is explainable as self-induced cosmic energy brought to visible light by their 'spiritual purity'—that is, by their lack of interfering vibrations from confused thought. Enlightenment reveals that what is most deeply personal is also most universal." [2] C. G. Jung writes, "The feeling for the infinite . . . can be attained only if we . . . are [conscious] of our narrow confinement in the self. In knowing ourselves to be . . . ultimately limited . . . we possess also the capacity for becoming conscious of the infinite." [3] In her book *Mysticism*, Evelyn Underhill distinguishes three stages on the way to enlightenment: the awakening of the Self, the purification of the self, and *then* the illumination of the self.

We must not be discouraged if the thought habits of a lifetime are so hard to erase that we sometimes echo the biblical cry, "Lord, I believe; help thou mine unbelief (Mark 9:24, KJV)." As in the parable of the frogs in the milk can, the continual kicking of our agitated reading and discussion is churning a substantial base from which we will at the magic moment leap into the larger universe.

In Condition Seven we identified three immediate needs: *wisdom* for our remaining earth life, *love* of the cosmic life-in-God in his joyous creativity, and *patience* for living the difficult local-and-cosmic life of the interim years. Then we *humbly* (any trace of arrogance or intellectual pride ruined everything) attempted to discover and cultivate the essential higher values that would supply these needs.

In earth relationships we took our stand on simple friendliness. In the life of the mind we found that books were our mainstay. Language was the great gift of the Creator uniquely bestowed on humanity, and books can carry the finest cargo of language. They fed our minds, fired our enthusiasm, sparked and enlivened the discussions at our meetings, and poured into us a stream of strength distilled from exalted minds and spirits.

As for our first need—wisdom for our remaining earth life— we made the acquaintance of a book that has become a classic for the seeker after meaning in life, William James's *Varieties of Religious Experience*. Here we had the benefit of following one of the finest minds America had produced as it struggled with the same kinds of problems we ourselves were trying to puzzle through. Today's standard psychology texts cite William James as one of the four founders of modern psychology, the others being Wilhelm Wundt, John Dewey, and Sigmund Freud.

James began his career as a sage with a professorship in physiology at Harvard Medical School. He then became a professor of psychology and crowned this phase of his career with the great two-volume *Principles of Psychology*, called by Columbia University's distinguished professor Jacques Barzun "a classic treatise standing to this day as a landmark in the history of psychology." It was immediately recognized in world centers of learning as an epoch-making new departure. But James tired of psychology, calling it "a *little* science" which precluded any serious consideration of man's cosmic origin, function, and ultimate purpose. He became a professor of philosophy and in 1902 presented his research and thought in the Gifford lectures at the University of Edinburgh. These twenty lectures were published in book form (today available as a widely read paperback) under the title *Varieties of Religious Experience*.

He wrote in the *Varieties:*

There is a state of mind known to religious men, but to no others, in which the will to assert ourselves and hold our own has been displaced by a willingness to close our mouths and be as nothing in the floods and waterspouts of God. In this state of mind, what we most dreaded has become the habitation of our safety, and the hour of our mortal death has turned into our spiritual birthday. The time for tension in our soul is over, and that of happy relaxation, of calm deep breathing, of an eternal present, with no discordant future to be anxious about, has arrived.[4]

C. G. Jung, because he was the first and is still the most profound writer to give deep thought to the inner psychic landscape of aging, has become a kind of patron saint of The Last Third Club. He left two books that have given us steady insight and support, *Modern Man in Search of a Soul* and *Memories, Dreams, Reflections*. In the former book he sketched the general psychic structure of human experience, reviewed the special difficulties of contemporary industrial man, pinpointed the unique emotional and spiritual challenges of aging, and hinted at appropriate solutions. "Man has never yet been able singlehanded to hold his own against the powers of darkness," he concluded in the former work. He "has always stood in need of the spiritual help which each individual's own religion held out to him." [5]

In the latter volume, an informal autobiography, he told in intimate detail how he himself coped with some of the very problems that now assail us. In summary, he wrote:

When Lao-tzu says: "All are clear, I alone am clouded," he is expressing what I now feel in advanced old age. Lao-tzu is the example of a man with superior insight who has seen and experienced worth and worthlessness, and who at the end of his life desires to return into his own being, into the eternal unknowable meaning. The archetype of the old man who has seen enough is eternally true. At every level of intelligence this type appears, and its lineaments are always the same, whether it be an old peasant or a great philosopher like Lao-tzu. This is old age, and a limitation. Yet there is so much that fills me: plants, animals, clouds, day and night, and the eternal in man. The more uncertain I have felt about myself, the more there has grown up in me a feeling of kinship with all things.[6]

Raynor Johnson, in his *Nurslings of Immortality*, has helped us immeasurably with his discussion of time and eternity and the overall nature of the universe as seen from the point of view of imaginative science and philosophy. Dr. Johnson, a Ph.D. from Oxford and the University of London, has been Master of Queen's College, Melbourne. While granting that "a microbe seeking to understand man might have less difficulty than man seeking to understand God," he nevertheless found, in the human and divine imaginations, a meeting place for the long-sought harmony and union:

God does not think, he imagines, and his imagining is reality. By imagining He creates, and this is essentially objective reality on every significant level. Divine Imagining has its "feeling" aspect—supreme Delight, Love and Beauty. We know how, in ourselves, there are moments of delight. The nature of Divine Imagining is radiant and fully reflective, to an extent which we can only faintly guess. The mystics who in rare moments have been granted some vision of Reality speak with one voice of this supreme Delight-Love-Beauty, to tell more of which words fail.[7]

The little book *Alcoholics Anonymous*—the raft which has rescued so many hundreds of thousands from drowning in the sea of one of modern man's most baffling and murderous diseases—has also held interest for many of us. This is not so much because alcoholism is a significant problem among us as because Alcoholics Anonymous, as one of history's outstanding demonstrations of the solution of "insoluble" life problems by spiritual means, is an inspiration to us. If men and women can be pulled out of the wreckage of advanced alcoholism and restored to radiant mental, spiritual, and physical health by such means, surely there is hope for such as us! "Half-measures availed us nothing," write these anonymous authors. "We stood at the turning-point. Without help it was too much for us. But there is one who has all power— that One is God. We asked His protection and care with complete abandon. Rarely have we seen a person fail who has thoroughly followed our path."

In the course of our inner speculations we do not let ourselves forget the outer world. Its condition, the general condition of man, and moral responsibility toward the perennial issues are part of our lives. Books like Barry Commoner's statement on ecology, *Science and Survival*, and *The Limits to Growth*, by Prof. D. L. Meadows of the Massachusetts Institute of Technology, remind us that we are still very physical members of a species that for the time being dominates a very physical earth. As part of our acquisition of higher values we need to know enough about immediate earth conditions to take a wise position on the crucial issues. Such books have been an important aid toward this end.

But books alone can never do the whole job. Nobody can read everything. Everybody can read something, however, and it's surprising how much helpful information gets passed around when a group of habitual readers gets together to talk about what they've been reading and evaluate it in the light of their own experience. Thus we say that not only through reading but also through discussion and reflection do we humbly attempt to discover and cultivate those higher values so essential to our new life—wisdom, cosmic love, patience, and simple friendliness.

NINE

Having thus gained a clearer perspective on life's major phases, we have steadfastly sought the wisdom it is the business of life's later years to acquire and preserve.

The key word in Condition Nine is "steadfastly." There is no tentative note here; we're beginning to be more certain of our ground. Step Eight was a humble search for the new values essential to our new life. We didn't yet know what those values might turn out to be; we were on a voyage of search and discovery. Now, in Condition Nine, it is perfectly clear in our minds that the goals of the first half of life are done for—we've had it with all that. It is equally clear, now that we've begun to grasp the evolutionary functions of life's major phases, that the most serious business of our life lies before us.

We have a clear conception of our life situation and we know what we're looking for: wisdom. We could say, with Sophocles, "There is no happiness where there is no wisdom," and add with him, "Proud men [and women!] in their maturer years must learn to be wise."

But gaining wisdom, we soon discovered, was a tricky thing. The moment we began to say to ourselves, "Now I am wise," we lost whatever modicum of wisdom we might have had! Socrates, the prototypic wise man of Greek antiquity, never considered himself wise. "They call me the wisest man in Athens, yet all I ever do is ask questions." Jesus of Nazareth made no claims to wisdom. "I only do," he said, "what I see my father do."

Wisdom is a mysterious combination of knowledge

83

and insight. There is nothing we can do about sharpening our insight but continue our ever-deepening daily meditations. There *is* something we can do about improving our knowledge: we can read, discuss, reflect, and open-mindedly listen. Reflection and meditation on what we read and hear will—experience has taught us—flavor our knowledge with insight and turn part of it into wisdom. As wisdom it will become radiant, and as radiance it will have a beneficial effect, not only on our own sense of well-being and essential worth but also on the wider earth life of which we're still a part.

As Dr. Jung implied when he observed that people cannot know infinity except from the viewpoint of the limited self, an important part of wisdom is humility. We begin each day on the assumption that we know nothing. We never say, "Now I am going to do the wise thing" (our "wisdom" has too often turned out to be foolishness!). We merely ask ourselves "Is it wise?" and then act on our best insight, never knowing whether we have acted wisely until enough time has gone by to observe and reflect upon the results of the action. We are convinced that an essential factor in the acquisition of wisdom is time.

Personal wisdom is always relative. Proverbs, mottoes, and adages—"Don't cut off your nose to spite your face," "Don't saw off the limb you're standing on," and so on—cannot be trusted. There may be times in our journey toward Self-realization when we'll find we'd have a *better* face if we lopped off some cherished bit of pride, prejudice, or tribal arrogance and substituted a new feature—perhaps global or cosmic tolerance or the humility of Self. There may be times when it would be *beneficial to* saw off the rotten limb on which we've been standing (or, more accurately, teetering) and trust our full weight to one of the growing spiritual limbs of the divine living tree. We have resolutely put behind us the conventional platitudes of the proud-grandparent senior-citizen cult. We will not burden one another with tiresome accounts of past triumphs in love or commerce, or competitively list the places we've visited, or review the restaurants where we've eaten or the bargains we've found, or rehearse once more our forthcoming visits to our adorable grandchildren or proclaim their remarkable achievements or lament their precious vagaries. We don't have time for this kind of senile nonsense; the evolutionary business of the last third of life is too pressing.

Yes, the lodestone word of Condition Nine is "steadfastly." By this word we steer our course, which we know in advance will be neither smooth nor easy nor free from fog, sleet, and rough weather. We are constructing a mature philosophy for the final years of life out of the wreckage of the catch phrases that governed our earlier years. This means rebuilding our operating psychology from scratch.

This, considering the systematic miseducation we've all been subjected to, is no small job. One of our members commented as follows on the size of the corrective task: "As a kid, my impression was that great-grandfather was the first human being. After him came George Washington. Then, more or less in this order, came Jesus Christ, the Pilgrims, the pioneers, and Adam-and-Eve, who produced all the families except great-grandfather's. History began in 1776. Before that there were only cavemen, dinosaurs, and the British, who were mean devils to the last man."

Any normally impressionable child might come out of his first years of family, church, and public "education" with a similar hash. The same member who commented in this way on his early impressions added, "I learned elementary solar-system astronomy after I got to college, and then only after a knockdown battle with the academic authorities in charge of my specialized curriculum."

Someday, we hope, children will be taught the truth of the human condition in orderly and comprehensible sequence. Small children have a spontaneous attraction to the great natural facts of existence—to stars, sun, and moon; to water, earth, and hills; to flowers and trees; to birds and animals. There is no reason why they can't be taught basic astronomy in kindergarten—"first came the galaxies, like our Milky Way, and with them the stars, like our sun, and with them the planets, like our earth and morning and evening stars, and with them the moons, like our moon." Geological and biological evolution would be introduced in the first grade; anthropology and cultural evolution in the second; the rise of the great civilizations and reasons for their fall in the third; major world nationalisms in the fourth; world cohesive and splintering trends in the fifth; efforts of the local tribalism to emancipate itself in the sixth; man's great liberating arts and ideas in the seventh; and, in the eighth, an introduction to man's search for the personal meaning of his individual life. Only in the ninth grade, with these great universals well implanted, would it be considered prudent to expose the pupils to the kinds of tribalistic specializations that will all too soon make their bids to swallow mind and soul. Higher education, at the undergraduate level, would concern itself exclusively with planetary management, with majors in the ecological, esthetic, cultural, and industrial areas of concentration after two full years of general background. Only at the postgraduate level would further specialization be advised.

But such reforms cannot come in time to help us. We must therefore make it our main later-life task to reeducate ourselves as we should have been educated in the first place. This will inevitably bring us some painful surprises. Not the least will be the discovery of the power of those remote figures we once called Mommy and Daddy. Every time we try to change an outmoded but still deeply entrenched idea, we run into the long arm and strong hand of their influence. "Mom said this was true"—and said it about something that turned out to be obviously *untrue*—can face us with the need for an abrupt and wrenching adjustment. "Dad did it so it must be right"—about something clearly *not* right—can do the same.

Here is where we must be steadfast, remembering that our bodies are spiritualizations of the physical environment—earth, sun, and local stellar cosmos—our minds and Selves are our windows on the divinely imagined universe. There will be times of mental confusion while we try to choose between this old value and that new one. At such times, our experience suggests, the course of wisdom is to seize any appropriate straw—even if it's only a hackneyed slogan or an ancient prayer—until the dust storm settles and we can see clearly again. We cannot lift ourselves; help must come from outside or we flounder.

These are some of the emergency phrases used successfully by other stressed group seekers as beacon lights, bringing concentrated group experience instantly to bear: "First things first" as a corrective for inability to concentrate; "Easy does it" for impatience; "Live and let live" for difficulty in achieving that human imperative we call forgiveness; "It takes all kinds" as an aid toward the ideal we have set ourselves and named "cosmic simple friendliness." A well-known prayer by Reinhold Niebuhr runs:

O God, give me the serenity
    to accept what cannot be changed—
Give me the courage to change what can be changed—
And the wisdom to know the one from the other.

This prayer has proved to be a useful stepping-stone toward freedom from deep-seated resentment. The Lord's Prayer has been found by many to be an unfailing restorer of lost perspective. An adaptation of a famous prayer by Francis of Assisi that goes "God help me seek to understand rather than to be understood, to love rather than to be loved, to comfort rather than to be comforted, to serve rather than to be served," often puts us back on a lost road to tolerance. We can't lift ourselves by our own earlobes or raise our spiritual level without some purchase on a base outside ourselves. Often, during a heavy blow, these prayers and slogans have put our feet back on the spiritual escalator.

"Don't cut off the branch you're standing on," as we mentioned earlier, is a double-edged maxim whose meaning can be so ambiguous as to render it of little use in problems of our individual psyches. When dealing with the mass behavior of all mankind, however, its meaning is unequivocal. All humans, of all faiths, colors, tribes, and political persuasions, breathe from a single thin envelope of air which is supplied with oxygen by the "living" (i.e., life-sustaining) oceans (land foliage, a secondary oxygen source, is not adequate alone). Biologically dead oceans cannot supply oxygen. By accidental and deliberate oil discharges, systematic chemical pollution, and overfishing, we are killing the oceans. This is indeed sawing off the limb on which all mankind stands. Whether he be capitalist, Communist, politically inert, Catholic, Protestant, atheist, Jew, Muslim, Buddhist, Orthodox, male, female, young, old, white, yellow, black, brown, red, or from the northern or southern regions of any nation or hemisphere, all will die if the oceans cease producing oxygen.

The time when this and other ecological threats will be felt is not far off. The first comprehensive attempt to measure the effect of technology on human life was begun in 1968 by Aurelio Peccei, an Italian industrialist and economist. Peccei recruited seventy-five businessmen and scientists of world reputation as members of "The Club of Rome." With $250,000 donated by the Volkswagen Corporation, a computer study of "the predicament of mankind" was begun at the Massachusetts Institute of Technology. The survey was completed in 1972, and the results are now under serious discussion at conference tables all around the world.

The decisive factor is an ominous trend which statisticians call exponential increase. Unlike linear increase, which is a simple sequence of 1, 2, 3, 4, 5, exponential increase goes 1, 2, 4, 8, 16, 32—doubling every period. As applied to human population (doubling every thirty years) world population in 1990 will be eight times what it was in 1900—and in 2020 will be *sixteen* times the 1900 figure—and in 2050 *thirty-two* times! At this rate the theoretical date when there would be Standing Room Only on the earth is approaching with unsuspected speed. But other calamities will overtake mankind long before the SRO stage is reached if the species does not soon begin to control its numbers. Population, production, resource extraction, and pollution are all increasing exponentially. Using actual figures of growth from 1900 to 1970 and then projecting them by computer into the future, the Club of Rome study indicates calamitous breakdowns in all major aspects of the world socioeconomic system not long after the year 2000. Mitigating assumptions (such as an increase in beneficial technological innovation) may somewhat delay the timing; but if we continue our present technological practices, disaster is inevitable.

This, in the context of Condition Nine, is simple knowledge. It is not yet wisdom, and will not become so until it has had long exposure to meditation, intuition, reflection, and discussion. What does one do, as an individual, in the presence of such knowledge? One asks one's self, "What would be the wise thing?" Then, thoroughly understanding that one might be wrong whatever one does, one acts according to the answers that come to him after reflection. What one does is always an individual decision. The Last Third Club does not make policy; each member speaks for himself alone. Since this is a fairly typical decision problem, we asked one of our members, as a demonstration, to work out an answer to it. Carefully noting that it is only one individual's answer, we here print his response:

The problem really has three components: spiritual, mental, and physical. On the spiritual plane, the ominously approaching crisis of earth existence reinforces my spiritual feeling that mankind is a brotherhood-sisterhood which stands or falls as one. Reflection on it deepened my sympathy for all humans and all earth creatures. It furthered my dislike of all splintering tribalisms and strengthened my earlier conviction that "the highest conscious achievement of earth life is universal simple friendliness."

On the mental plane, I found reinforcement of an already established conviction of mine that the universe is essentially mental in nature, hence responds to mental activity. If our air, land, and water are polluted it is only because our thinking is polluted. Clear thinking will bring clear air and water; fertile thinking will bring fertile land. We know how to recycle our sewage, garbage, and wastes so they can enrich the depleted land while clearing the waters—all we have to do now is think this knowledge into action. It then becomes wisdom—the wisdom that can save the earth and everything that lives on it.

On the physical plane, I concluded there was not much I could do beyond contributing to ecology-oriented organizations as my resources allowed, talking it up when chance threw a receptive listener into my path, supporting ecology-conscious political candidates, and praying for further guidance.

Is this "wisdom"? We do not claim so. Wisdom, we think, is acquired by the habitual practice of humbly asking appropriate questions, conscientiously reflecting and meditating on the answers we seek and find, and a steadfast continued seeking. We have made such seeking the absorbing preoccupation of our later years.

Ten

These steps have brought an awareness of cosmic dimensions we had not hitherto explored and have led us into the realm of deep spiritual experience.

It would be hard to find a man more thoroughly grounded in hardheaded, thoroughly materialistic, computerized, down-to-business, modern practical science than Edgar Mitchell, commander of Apollo 14's lunar module. After taking a doctoral degree in science at the Massachusetts Institute of Technology he served as an engineer, a test pilot, a management specialist, and a graduate instructor at M.I.T., before becoming an astronaut.

Now in his forties, he seriously questions the validity of the basic assumptions of the same materialistic science he spent so many years becoming expert in. He writes:

Some years ago I began searching for concepts that would explain and give meaning to life. I looked into many things, including spirit communication and other phenomena related to parapsychology. To my surprise, disbelief about the validity of these occurrences began melting away. I had spent years learning the objective methods of science. As one dedicated to decision-making on the basis of empirical evidence and objective experiment, it was impossible for me to avoid the clear implication that if consciousness can *operate* independently of the body, perhaps it can also *exist* independently of the body and survive death.

There now seemed to be sound reason for religious belief—a rational basis for explaining why people throughout history have persisted in claiming a spiritual foundation to the physical world. I am now convinced that "death" is a transition to continued life.

This changes not only our attitude toward death but also our attitude toward life.

Man must rise from his present ego-centered consciousness to sense his intimate participation in the planet's functioning, and beyond that, in the functioning of the universe. Man must find universal attunement, starting within himself and proceeding outward through his relation with the cosmos. Only thus can the people of the planet find personal fulfillment, peace and harmony.[1]

Dr. Mitchell is by no means alone in expressing this cosmic point of view among his fellow scientists. Dr. Charles Tart, professor of psychology at the University of California at Davis, finds that a great many scientists are growing restless under the old materialistic rigidities of thought. In a determined effort to bring actual parapsychological events within the purview of formal science, they are looking toward entirely new dimensions of consciousness. Writing in the authoritative magazine *Science*, official journal of the American Association for the Advancement of Science, Professor Tart finds that "mature scientists in increasing numbers are turning to meditation" and other means of entering the more extensive and otherwise altered states of consciousness (ASC).

The phenomena encountered in these ASC's provide more satisfaction and are more relevant to the formulation of philosophies of life and deciding upon appropriate ways of living, than "pure reason." My own impressions are that very large numbers of scientists are now personally exploring ASC's.[2]

These are very recent statements. We pioneers of The Last Third Club had reached parallel conclusions many years earlier by very different routes. At the time we first took our positions of firm belief in life after death and the potent activity of Spirit, we were regarded as being quite unscientific and perhaps a little far out. We have here quoted Drs. Mitchell and Tart as part of a mounting body of evidence that science is at last beginning to swing away from the rigid materialism that has stifled it for the past three centuries. It is no longer unscientific to believe in infinity (Jung), in psychic phenomena, in the life beyond death, in God. Science is at last beginning to catch up with us!

Not that we would have greatly minded if it hadn't. The experienced reality of the dimensions that began to open to us in Condition Ten was its own conclusive evidence. In introducing newcomers to the true forces and facts of life, however, we prefer to quote scientific authority rather than our own private experience whenever we can. They are often in complete agreement, but to still earth-minded strangers the word of science is more persuasive. And recent scientific evidence is accumulating most convincingly.

Statements of the kind we have quoted, which are becoming more and more frequent among men of science, mark the beginning of a profound change in the intellectual climate of modern man. It is in essence a reaffirmation of the central truths of the great religions. But it has been arrived at not through a turning backward to the beliefs of an earlier day but by driving forward with true scientific insight toward the central nature of cosmic existence.

When we return to the world's great religious writings after having acquired a little parapsychological insight, we find them to be made up mostly of simple records of the great psychics of recorded history. They are, in modern terms, compendiums of well-witnessed parapsychological case histories. They are *not* unique historical events but demonstrations of forces eternally active in daily life. The same forces active then are active now, and the same sorts of phenomena are daily being demonstrated.

The Old Testament range of psychic ability is vast. Moses was what today would be called a "psychic" or "sensitive." He was clairaudient (heard voices) and produced independent writing. Abraham heard voices, went into trances and had meaningful visions. Jacob manifested discarnates physically and had conversations with them. Joseph was powerfully precognitive and could interpret dreams. Balaam was clairvoyant and clairaudient, as was Gideon. Elisha was precognitive. Elijah had all these powers and also could produce apports—instant transport of objects to designated and sometimes distant points, as in the New Testament case of the loaves and the fishes. (Apports are being produced by a powerful medium today under laboratory conditions at Stanford University.)

Jesus of Nazareth was a divenly inspired teacher on a cosmic evolutionary mission. He was also—as another great psychic, John the Baptist, immediately saw—a psychic of very great stature. Jesus' recorded "miracles" (a misnomer, since these events are produced according to natural laws still inadequately studied) are without exception in categories of events regularly reported in modern psychical research. Most striking, perhaps, are the apports—appearances, like the wine at Cana, the loaves at the convocation, the coin in the fish's mouth to appease the tax collector— of materials that had not been there an instant before. Numerous examples, one of them an emergence of coins from the sea quite in the New Testament manner, are recorded in our own time. The famous episode of walking on the water is a case of levitation, a phenomenon known to thousands of contemporary families as regards gravity-defying movement of physical objects. A famous twentieth-century demonstrator of self-levitation of the human body was the Italian monk Father Pio. The Israeli sensitive Uri Geller is demonstrating laboratory levitations of physical objects as I write. Telekinesis, the movement of physical objects by purely mental means, is one of the most common occurrences of the physical type today. The rolling of the stone from the tomb of Jesus was a New Testament example of TK. Full material-izations and dematerializations (the Resurrection and later appearances of Jesus) have never been common but have been reliably witnessed in our own time. The withering-of-the-fig-tree type of influence on plants has been duplicated in substance, under the most rigid scientific control. That Jesus was clairvoyant is indi-cated by the ease with which he took in the life situa-tion of the woman of Samaria (this type of clairvoy-ance is one of the most widely demonstrated in psychic circles today). That Jesus was precognitive and a sensitive telepathic receiver—gifts not unusual among earth's present population—is shown by his prediction of his own execution and by his knowledge of what his disciples were thinking. As for his healing "miracles," any modern hospital possessing a psychically oriented chaplain—and there are many such—can produce medically attested records of spontaneous healings almost as astonishing. The little book *The Light That Heals*, reviewed in Appendix IV of this book, covers a wide range of the psychic healings and methods now in common use.

We have said little about the great psychics of the Eastern tradition—the legendary Krishna, Lao-tzu, Buddha, Shankara—or of the Sufis of Islam, or of the great sensitives of Persia, or of Egypt, or of Peru, or of "primitive" peoples. The testimony of all is unanimous and to the same point: there is more to the universe than can ever be known through the five physical senses or any instrumentation of them. In the Christian tradition, the evidence continues from where the New Testament left off. A few great psychics survived all hazards and are remembered as saints. The thirteenth century brought Francis of Assisi, with his levitations, ecstatic visions, and, at the last, his stigmata. The fifteenth century produced Joan—later *Saint* Joan—of Arc, who was clairvoyant, clairaudient, and precognitive. The abilities of St. Teresa of Avila, a Roman Catholic nun who lived in Spain in the sixteenth century, included spirit writing, automatic writing, clairaudience, levitation, materialization, and an unusually acute intelligence.

Protestants have also produced numerous gifted psychics. In seventeenth-century England, George Fox heard voices, gave himself over to the guidance of an Inner Light, held meetings so packed with psychic power that the building shook, experienced visions, and predicted the future. Fox foresaw the Revolution of 1688 and the Great Fire of London. He was clairvoyant, went into trance, and was a healer. The nineteenth-century Alexander Campbell, cofounder of the Disciples of Christ, had psychic ability that expressed itself in visions and foreknowledge. All these gifts have been in the public eye throughout the twentieth century. The prophecies of more recent American sensitives—particularly Arthur Ford and Edgar Cayce —are well known. Contemporary American spiritual healers include Norbu Chen, an American who studied in China and developed a phenomenal ability to heal psychically. Chen's healing gift is now being studied scientifically.

The new support from scientific quarters—precincts which until recently had been dogmatically atheistic —does not, of course, relieve us of our personal struggle to comprehend ourselves and the universe of which we are a part. It only helps us a little in being steadfast, by giving us one more prop of support, always welcome when one is working to maintain a spiritual world view in a materialist world. Any effort toward spiritual growth must always work against an undertow of old imprint, the weight of the doubting masses, and the earthly attachments and desires of our own selves. We tend forever to try to "build a house" on a life that is really a bridge to be crossed, not a lot to be settled on. The seekers of all ages have had the struggle experience and have given it a name, "the dark night of the soul." These attacks of doubt can be agonizing—but the agony passes. Jesus compared it to childbirth: "When a woman is in travail she has sorrow, . . . but when she is delivered of the child, she no longer remembers the anguish, for joy (John 16:21)." "Tiger! tiger! burning bright in the forests of the night," is how the poet Blake put it; in the depths of our collective unconscious lives the tiger of our predatory human past, to reach for us as long as we live.

But our tigerish inheritance loses its force as we evolve toward the simple friendliness of fourth-state, nonpredatory, humanistic, cosmically oriented man. In this evolution we utilize every mental force that comes to us in our own behalf, and we hold to it with our utmost powers of belief. It is trusted imagination, psychic experience, and belief that open to us the reality of the larger dimensions. This is the truth that led Jesus to say to the seekers of his own day, "This is the work of God, that you believe in him whom he has sent (John 6:29)." When science aids in this belief, so much the better; when science hinders, we hold to evident truth and let science go until it learns more. Thus, as we experience more and more of our own inward life, we come more and more to trust our inward insights and intuitions.

Does this mean that we are all likely to become great psychics, speaking with spirits, moving objects by thought, healing by touch, and all the rest of it? Probably not. Very few of us regard ourselves as having special psychic gifts in any notable degree. But by the same token there are very few of us who have *not* had a deeply moving spiritual experience of some kind. Sometimes it may take the form of a startling answer to prayer. Sometimes it may be a powerful hunch that turns out to be veridical. Sometimes it is an experience of ecstasy, or of a spontaneous healing, or of cosmic love, or perhaps it is simply the quiet entry into our lives of a new serenity and confidence concerning both the near and the far future. We cannot predict what any individual experience may be, but all experiences of this kind have these factors in common: they bring us a new awareness of vast cosmic dimensions yet to be explored and a definite knowledge of having entered a realm of deep spiritual experience.

The experience of a daily transcendental joy in meditation, however brief it may be, however fleeting, transforms our lives and prepares us for a creative death. Pain is endured and forgotten. We now know we are loved, not because we are virtuous and deserving but simply because it is God's nature to love us. We have experienced the meaning of "God is Love." From time to time we experience significant dreams and accurate intuitions. We have encounters "by accident" whose meaning seems to go far beyond accident or chance. We have fortuitous lessons and insights, surprising healings and recoveries, a new radius and radiance of friendship, a daily joy in simple things, an occasional ecstasy in meditation so transforming that we no longer need to labor intellectually over the issue of life beyond death, since we now know the reality of eternity and the certainty of the kingdom of heaven—we have been there. These are some of the hallmarks of Condition Ten.

Eleven

Though aware that the workaday world undervalues spiritual wisdom, we offer what we have of it when asked.

"In every critical period of life an inner birth process takes place," wrote the psychiatrist Franz Winkler. "Whether its fruits will ripen and mature, or die, or grow into monstrosities, depends on wisdom and free will. Evolution requires a supreme effort of will." [1]

The governing thought of Condition Eleven is this very "supreme effort of will." According to the thoroughness with which we have lived out the preceding Conditions, we are now prepared to reenter the world of action—but with an entirely new outlook and freed of many of our old and restricting habits. "Even the best of habits," remarked Dr. Winkler in his book *Man, The Bridge Between Two Worlds*, "are no more than casts into which one's will may flow. Essentially rigid, and truly useful only as props for routine affairs, they must be overcome—regardless of whether they are good or bad—whenever an act of free will is required." [2]

The previous Conditions have broken the grip of our strongest habits to the extent that we are now beginning to live as free human beings instead of tribe-conditioned robots. Freed from the narrow slot of gain-oriented tasks and predilections, we have begun a new life in an infinite universe of divine thought, imagination, and spirit. For most of our lives we have worked for our own or somebody else's habits. From now on we will either have our habits work for us, toward some higher end than mere repetition, or we will part company with them. To live in this new way will call for an unshakable decision and a firm effort of will. In Condition Eleven we are ready to make that decision and put forth that effort of will.

We have come to see existence almost as a new religion, arising out of and encompassing whatever our old one—or lack of one—may have been. The general outlines of the new edifice are already beginning to show themselves. The development is advancing in two prongs—one earthly, outward, and practical, the other inward, imaginative, and spiritual.

From now until the time of our transition we will be living abundantly in both these worlds. The earthly physical branch is beginning to make itself known under the name of ecology. At no time since the beginning of the industrial revolution have so many thoughtful people been so concerned about the relation of man to his total environment. Water, air, and fertile earth, industrial man is beginning to relearn, are the stuff from which his earth body is made. Unless they are plentifully available in pure form, his earth body will perish. With this understanding he is recapturing some of the knowledge he once possessed, but had forgotten, and approaching his environment with a new caution and respect. He is rediscovering the fact that the biosphere is not inert but is conscious. It reacts to him in a mutual dependency.

Man is at last grasping the meaning of the Bible's word that he has "dominion" on earth. The Cosmic Creative Intelligence is sharing with him the work of creative evolution on earth and has made him earth's administrator. Physically, ecologists like Prof. F. A. Brown (of Northwestern University and the U.S. Marine Biology Laboratory at Woods Hole) are beginning to realize that the environment—the *physical* environment—affecting man extends far beyond earth, moon, and sun and their gravitational fields. Man, in a strictly physical sense, is cosmic. Scientists had long assumed that creatures following seasonal, solar, and lunar rhythms learned about cyclic changes from the usual sensual sources—weather, water movements, sunshine. Professor Brown began years ago to watch living creatures in sealed quarters where environmental factors such as barometric pressure, temperature, illumination, and humidity were always the same. To Brown's surprise, the confined creatures maintained their rhythms. Oysters, when moved a thousand miles from their native beaches, timed their opening and closing to what the tides would have been had the sea extended that far inland. Potato buds followed the seasons as faithfully as potatoes living outdoors, somehow, though in perpetual artificial twilight, they always knew the position of the sun. How they came by this knowledge is one of the unsolved mysteries of organic life. Brown established that living creatures react to forces from outside the earth. Some of these forces operate, in Brown's words, "at energy levels so low that we have hitherto considered the organisms completely oblivious to them. There are still unknown temporal and spacial, subtle and pervasive forces influencing the behavior of living things." [3]

At the same time that man's awareness of local and outer space has been extended, so has his depth-psychological experience—his exploration of inner space. Once this psychic area is opened, its relatedness to the physical realm becomes apparent. Man and the living creatures of earth are seen as products of the Cosmic Creative Intelligence—the divine imagination. The power of the creative imagination, both human and divine, over physical things is clear. Physical and psychical are seen to be one. The great project of creation is seen to be evolution, not just of physical shapes, colors, activities, and forms but of consciousness, understanding, compassion, the ability to create and maintain intricate harmonies, the capacity to comprehend. As this comprehension establishes its beachhead in us, the outlines of the "many mansions" come into view—universe upon universe of soul space to be explored, understood, and mastered. Our mustard seed is spreading its branches and turning into a shade tree.

This is the business of our meditative life, our reading life, our life of fellowship within The Last Third Club. But we also have another life to lead—practical, realistic, useful, very much in the here-and-now—and it is to this life that a firm effort of our will must now be applied.

Here we encounter the full strength of that earthbound power we have named force of habit. All our lives, the paradigms of our competitive, survival-in-the-tribe, prestige-oriented behavior have been the practical Man and the Practical Woman. The Man (or Woman) at the Top (by tribal custom the only place to aspire to) always has an element of hardness and ruthlessness about him. He is "practical," meaning that he deals only in tangibles. Anything intangible, unless it can be seen ultimately to produce tangibles, is brushed aside because it is probably fuzzy, dreamy, and impractical.

Such ruthless practicality, history has been trying to tell us for a number of centuries now, does not work out very well. Other nations have their hard guys at the top too, and each tribe is convinced that its own national brand of hardness has to be the hardest of all. The ultimate tragedy of the Practical Man is that he is impractical. Because his calculations always omit certain subtle and unknown forces, they carry him to his own destruction.

This is daily becoming a more and more visible fact. "Practical" men are on the very brink of destroying, by the poisons they release through their presumably practical activities, the very environment that sustains them. Unless they suddenly become practical enough to curb themselves in time, practical men and women will produce, in the next thirty years, more children than were born in the preceding million years. Such overproduction—and its resulting overcrowding and overburdening earth's limited resources—would certainly mean the end of human life as we have known it and possibly the end of all human life in its physical form. To bring on worldwide famines, immeasurable human suffering, and probable extinction does not seem so very practical. The hard guy is obsolete. The need of our time is for men and women who have the vision to think, feel, plan, and live—here and now—in the light of the ultimate extensions of human and cosmic insight.

But what, we must now ask ourselves, can such people contribute to an essentially predatory, gain-oriented society? What chance have peace and harmony in an atmosphere of fear, combat, and ruthless indifference to human need? How can you get cocky young predators who think they know everything to listen to the voice of wisdom—even assuming one could speak with that voice? These are our problems, these the big questions of reentry. Each individual, of course, must find his own answers according to his own personal life equation. It is one of our rules that no one speaks in the name of The Last Third Club; all any individual can do is contribute his personal experience to its reservoir of experience.

This, however, we who are in Condition Eleven accept as an axiom: God will never run out of resources. Even if the young predators should destroy the planet and everything in it (as a powerful consensus of them seem bent on doing) we will not believe that the Power who has created billions of galaxies *that we know of*, each containing billions of stars, around each of which whirl uncounted planets—we will not believe that such a creative Power has been finally defeated by willful men and women.

Short of this, and while there is time (the final destruction is, after all, not yet upon us), there is much we can do.

So many of our members have come up with successful solutions to the what-to-do-in-the-world problem that we are able to identify certain guiding principles. The main ones are service, compassion, and peace. Since we have come to regard this world as a bridge we are crossing on our way to another, we don't want to involve ourselves in anything that would hamper our ultimate spiritual progress. But while we still have unused energy, we do want to involve ourselves in *some*thing. The only taboo is that whatever we do must not interfere with our striving to achieve universal simple friendliness. We avoid activity that would draw us back into the predatory-competitive level of existence and cancel out our evolutionary gains. So long as our guiding motives are peaceful, compassionate, and service-oriented we are on safe ground—even if our activities should turn out, as a by-product, to be gainful. Due to the opening of the spiritual dimension in us, we are now creatures of two worlds. We cannot hurry our progress, much as we want to. If we're still here there's something for us to do that makes sense; all we have to do is find out what it is.

Whatever this may turn out to be, the basic conditions of our occupation will be different from what they were before. We are no longer exclusively *dependent* on our occupations. Even if *all* the props of this world should collapse, including the financial prop, we still have the infinite resources of the ultimate world to draw upon. Besides, our new motive is not primarily to get (though some getting may be advisable) but to give—to serve, in that cosmic friendliness we have come to think is the most valuable credential we can carry with us beyond our transition.

We will not expect, of course, to receive such friendliness in return. Most of the people we'll be working with are still predators, content with the predatory estate and its manners, so we may reasonably expect some differences in point of view. When these arise we never expect our viewpoint to prevail; the world is not yet that far along. Whether people are booing us or applauding us doesn't make a great deal of difference to us any more. All we're asking is to be of some small daily service in the world and to grow in the light that is emerging in ourselves. Though we enjoy discussions, we avoid arguments. When we keep our inner light alive, we have found, it radiates effectively even when our vocal cords are silent. On rare occasions people will ask us things. When they do, we give the best answers we have on hand, never counting on anything much to come of it.

The awkward age occupationally is the stretch of years beyond sixty-five. Many of us find ourselves as hale, hearty, and ready for work at sixty-six as we were at sixty-four, but our world situation is drastically changed. The welcome mat at the personnel office is no longer out. Some have been unable to endure this abrupt change; the casualties have been high. We have decided not to be casualties. We have learned from experience and observation that our best defenses are: (1) a readiness to serve even in a humble capacity, (2) advance mental preparation in the form of realistically accepting the facts of our situation, (3) a lively application of our imagination in thinking up things we might do, and (4) an unabashed willingness to endure a number of humiliating turn-downs until we finally find our slot.

"It seems to me," one of our members has remarked,

"that the hardest situation of all is that of the person who has no particular skills or talents that the world values, no worldly resources, and who has made no intellectual preparation for living out his later years. I was widowed at age sixty and had done nothing since I was a young girl but raise children, work at community-service volunteer jobs, and keep house. The only job I could find (and lucky to get that!) was cashier in a gift shop of a Chicago railroad terminal. I took seriously The Last Third Club's motto of 'service,' and it worked wonders. Just ringing up sales and making change can be pretty dull—but when I also made myself the station's unofficial ambassador to every confused and bewildered out-of-towner or foreigner who drifted past my counter, it changed everything. Never a day passed without being made worthwhile by helping somebody." She kept the job, incidentally, well into her seventies.

Restyling a former occupation to give it a service twist has solved the problem for a number of our members. One man, a chemical engineer with a midwestern illuminating-gas company, was retired at sixty-five. For a number of years he had been helping the neighborhood high schoolers with their science projects. When retirement year came, he went to the head of the school's science department and offered his services —gratis. The offer was accepted. "I did all kinds of odd jobs—tutoring youngsters who were having a hard time in science, making up solutions for use in the chemistry and biology labs, helping students with their workbooks and science projects." Soon the school began to employ him as a substitute when one of the regular teachers was absent. When his range was discovered (he could substitute equally well in math, chemistry, physics, or biology) he was made a teaching assistant—with pay. "I think a lot of people my age could do this kind of thing if they'd just try," he says. "You never know if you don't try." He's now seventy-four and still at his job.

We know of quite a number of these later-life self-made positions. One man, a management specialist, had always wanted to write poetry. When he retired at sixty-five he did so—and had a book of his poetry published, a rare and difficult thing even for established poets. "But," he said, "they publish so little poetry these days I couldn't keep at it full time and keep up my morale"—so he cast about for something else. As a lover of books he had always regretted seeing rare and beautifully bound books fall into disrepair. He took a course in bookbinding and is now on his way to founding his own one-man custom bookbinding service.

Another man we know, a nature lover, pointed out to his fellow townsmen the need for somebody to take an interest in the town's still beautiful but neglected trees. He invented the job of tree warden and got himself appointed to it. A retired storekeeper, all his life accustomed to keeping track of small change, gave his knack a service angle and became treasurer of his church—the only parishioner willing to spend time counting the children's Sunday school pennies. A Wall Street broker turned his lifelong interest in money into an appreciation of money as art. He found a job as clerk in a rare-coin shop and became expert enough to advise people on their coin collections. This kept him busy until his eyesight began to fail in his early eighties. Now, nearly blind, he keeps up with the new books and plays by listening to recordings for the blind. His service is to pass on what he's learned and thus keep alert and lively the minds of himself and the fellow guests in his retirement home.

Another man we know had spent his life making industrial films for commercial firms. After sixty-five he and his wife turned their cameras on a subject they'd long had a deep interest in—new and ancient religious trends around the world. Their enterprise is still small but very lively and growing. Another couple, having become deeply interested in meditation, discovered there was a shortage of teachers in their tradition of this practice. They studied under qualified auspices and became certified teachers of the technique they were interested in.

Volunteer work in a score of worthy organizations has filled the later-life occupational needs of many. Not the least in this kind of activity is The Last Third Club itself—and that brings us to Condition Twelve.

TWELVE

As our special responsibility, and as opportunity offers, we carry to others in the final third of life the heartening word that seniority can be joyous.

The Last Third Club aims to provide a friendly forum where men and women may share insight, information, and experience in living productively and creatively through life's later years. This book has been written to recount the experience of the founding members, thus far, and to express their conviction that living these years as closely as possible in accord with the Twelve Conditions has its advantages for all. So far we have been without formal organization, in existence but nameless and formless. Let us now acknowledge one another and act on our convictions. The spirit of Condition Twelve is action; we here set forth the simple means by which a path found by a few can be opened to many.

The "community forum" idea grew naturally out of our experience. Wherever the Twelve Conditions are mentioned there arises an eagerness to learn more about them—an eagerness born, sometimes, of desperation. The problem we cope with is large, worldwide, and urgent. There are twenty-one million people in the United States alone over the age of sixty-five, most of them in mild to acute bewilderment as to what to do with their lives. There are another forty-two million between forty-five and sixty-five who, according to Dr. Jung (and our own experience), should be "going to school" in preparation for living effectively with the new realities of the last third of life. Many of these older people are in extremity.

Sometimes the crackup comes while at work. One executive was found rigid, perspiring, and marble-eyed at his desk, unable for three tense, agonizing hours (he was approaching retirement age) to decide whether a certain piece of paper belonged in his "in" or his "out" basket. He was taken to the doctor's office in tears.

"Retirement syndrome" follows several characteristic and well-defined patterns, the most common of which is denial of plain fact. A man of sixty-three was asked to select and train his replacement in anticipation of his retirement at sixty-five. It took him six months to pick a successor—whom he pronounced unsatisfactory at the end of a year. Unable to imagine the company being able to get along without him, he still had not chosen a successor on retirement day. Instead he broke down, sinking into a profound depression from which a psychiatrist later made a belated effort to rescue him.

What happens to men in corporation offices happens as often to women in what one psychiatrist has called "the split-level trap." They too discover that, again quoting Dr. Jung, "for the aging person it is a duty and a necessity to give serious attention to himself." But "the promise of a life beyond . . . makes it possible for mortal man to live the second half of life with as much perseverance and aim as the first."[1]

We of The Last Third Club answer emphatically in the affirmative. "The serious problems of life," Dr. Jung continues, ". . . are never really solved. . . . The meaning . . . of a problem seems not to lie in its solution, but in our working at it incessantly. This alone preserves us from stultification. It is a fight waged within oneself as well as outside." [2]

During the past few years we have lived out the truth of this insight. We have had problems indeed and still have them. But working at them incessantly has produced—almost miraculously, seemingly as a by-product—a life that is singularly free from the terrors that once assailed us, full of moment-to-moment meaning and adventure, and even flavored from time to time with joy.

What shall we do with such a life? Hang on to it? Hoard it? Keep it to ourselves? Rather not! We must share it. By doing so we add immeasurably to its strength and richness and thereby increase our own pleasure in it. Besides that, there is the ineluctable pleasure of doing something in the world for somebody else—something that badly needs doing. Accordingly, we have worked out certain procedures for sharing.

The nuclear center of sharing we call a group. A group is two or more people who have come together for the purpose of seriously applying the Twelve Conditions of The Last Third Club to the actual living of the final third of their lives. Groups incline to grow, and when they do they need a secretary. If they become quite large they may also need a treasurer and a program chairman, but not much more in the way of officers. Our feeling is that organizational machinery should be kept to a minimum. Ideally, the group should own nothing, though in practical necessity it has to acquire and distribute its literature, keep up its correspondence, and answer inquiries. But it should never own substantial property. If, for example, clubhouse facilities should be desired, a separate commercial corporation should be formed, apart from The Last Third Club but available for those members who want it.

Officers should be rotated frequently—every six months —so that everyone has opportunity to serve and to exert influence. The Last Third Club avoids every kind of divisive entanglement in causes that might divert it from its central purpose, which is to enliven and inspire life's later years. Therefore it supports no issues or creeds and endorses nothing.

There is no requirement for membership but a desire to live the last third of life creatively and an interest in the club's Twelve Conditions as a means to that end. Neither members nor officers are authorized to speak authoritatively for the club. Each member's view is respected as that member's own opinion, not binding on any other members. When responding to requests for speakers to describe The Last Third Club and its work, members again speak from their own experience, observation, and reading. In keeping with a policy of emphasizing principles rather than personalities, members who speak publicly prefer to be introduced as "a member of The Last Third Club" rather than by name.

The Last Third Club does not seek financing, whether by public, private, religious, or community grants or any other source. It handles its own small expenses by pass-the-hat collections at its meetings. Members in financial straits are not expected to contribute. Each group functions independently of all other groups. A national secretary, should one be required, would function simply as a clearinghouse for information and contacts and as a source of literature. Public relations are low-key. We simply make known our existence and our aims, give cordial answers to all inquiries, and make welcome any whose life situation might lead them to consider joining us. Advertising does not go much beyond a brief "Last Third of Life Club Meets Wednesdays—Inquire Box 000" in the local weekly paper. Those who inquire may be mailed a copy of the Twelve Conditions and an invitation to attend the next meeting, perhaps followed up by a friendly phone call. Meeting announcements on appropriate bulletin boards, mail announcements to community centers, senior citizens' officers, retirement communities, service clubs, corporation personnel officers, and others who might be interested may also be arranged. Club-sponsored lectures for the general public are announced and advertised through the usual channels.

We bear in mind at all times that our stock-in-trade is simply our own experience. We can *relate* to older people because we have been through the same mill. We have met the crisis of aging and have more or less successfully fought some of its main battles. It is this, and nothing else, that creates the bond of fellowship and understanding that gives us our special influence with others who are only beginning to discover and cope with the new rules governing the last third of life.

The core of our work is our weekly meeting. Meetings should begin not much after eight and end not much after nine thirty—an hour and a half is enough. Promptness is important, both in opening and closing—the purpose is to stimulate and inspire, not to stupefy and exhaust. Since the Twelve Conditions of The Last Third Club are the pivot and basis of our later lives it may be wise to commit them to memory. Toward this end, some groups may open their meetings by reading aloud, in unison, the twelve conditions. Groups may observe a popular custom of closing with the Lord's Prayer. Meetings are essentially of three kinds: "condition and discussion," "formal two-speaker," and "outside guest lecturer." The first of these is likely to be the most usual, and even this requires a membership of six or seven in the local community. The first meetings, held before this book was written, were two men having lunch together once a week!

The "condition-and-discussion" meeting consists in one of the members speaking for half the period on his own efforts to apply one or more of the Conditions in his own life. In the second half of the evening, the floor is open for general discussion. Excerpts from the Conditions are read and commented on, experiences exchanged, problems discussed. Everybody present chips in with something to say about how things are going for *him*.

The speaker of the evening is, of course, the pump-primer. His talk is usually organized under four headings: (1) The life situation—personal, social, economic, and family—that first brought him to a realization that the problems of aging are serious, fundamental, potentially dangerous, and demanding incessant attention; (2) How he first learned of The Last Third Club and his early experience as a new member; (3) A review of his experience so far in applying the Twelve Conditions in his own living: which steps were most helpful, which he found most difficult, and so on; and (4) A rundown of what life gains he has made since his affiliation, topped off with a remark or two on his outlook for the future.

This kind of candid presentation of personal work in progress invariably reaches those present where they live and touches off a lively and heartening evening of fellowship. Decaffeinated coffee and wafers may be served as a further warmer before going home. When groups are small, meetings are likely to be held, in rotation, in members' homes. When the group is larger, meeting rooms may be found in a friendly church or community center.

Members, of course, take turns in being speaker of the evening. Nobody is asked to speak until he has been a member for three months. After that, speaking when one's turn comes is regarded as an obligation not lightly to be refused. When there are other groups nearby, a system of exchanging speakers can be arranged so that all groups can enjoy an infusion of new blood, new experience, new ideas.

For many new members there is a more or less

urgent need to talk privately with an understanding person about matters one might prefer not to present to the entire group. To meet this need a Senior Partner system may be put into effect. Each new member is assigned a guide or sponsor—man to man, woman to woman—called a Senior Partner (senior in Last Third Club experience, not necessarily in years), to be a confidant and friend while the new member is getting the hang of things. After a while, members tend to learn which of the group they are most compatible with and find their own friends. Once this has happened and the new member is firmly established in the group, the Senior Partner's special responsibility to him ceases.

Everybody needs someone special to confide in. Last Third Club members try to perform this service for each other. When one is chosen by a new member to receive special confidences, one regards the oath of secrecy as a sacred obligation. This is the sternest rule of The Last Third Club. One slip in the way of an item of gossip, one betrayal of a confidence, and the work of the entire group is jeopardized. The group is as strong as the mutual trust of its members.

Formal two-speaker meetings have not materialized as we go to press but seem to be a distinct possibility for the future. These may be held when a group wishes to reach out from its own small circle and invite two speakers—preferably a man and a woman—from neighboring or out-of-town groups to take over their program for the evening. Some of these visitors will have tales to tell of extraordinary vividness and helpfulness. In such evenings, each speaker would take thirty-five to forty minutes. In the time remaining, speakers would circulate with the members for informal chatting over decaffeinated coffee. The outside guest lecturer meeting would involve sponsoring some well-known and knowledgeable speaker on the psychological, emotional, and spiritual problems of aging, and turning over the entire evening to him.

As individual Last Third Club members, our goals in life are both inward and outward. Outwardly, we are becoming cosmophiles—lovers of the entire Creation—and we strive to express our change in that most exalted of human achievements, simple friendliness. Putting it another way, our outward thrust is toward our emergence from predator consciousness in the direction of ecology consciousness. Inwardly, through meditation, prayer, and continuing self-education, we are reaching toward cosmic consciousness—an awareness of the Whole, mental and physical, temporal and eternal, tangible and intangible. To say it another way, we strive to grow inwardly from tribal consciousness to cosmic consciousness.

Our progress toward these goals seems to proceed in units of comprehension, or plateaus, which we call "conditions of being," or just "the Conditions," or "the Steps." Since they are so central to our work, they will bear repeating:

1. We admit that death is closer for us who are in the last third of our lives than it is for the average person; that in this respect we are different from the majority of people.

2. We have come to see that, for those who are prepared, the eventual passage from this life can be a glory rather than a dread.

3. We have decided to use our remaining years primarily for this preparation.

4. We assert that the last third of life is given by nature for this high purpose; that it can illuminate all earlier experience in the joyous fulfillment of a rounded life.

5. We have resolved to give over our lives to Cosmic

Creative Intelligence as we individually name and experience this divine force.

6. Through regular morning and evening meditations, we are finding ourselves more and more in harmony with this transcendent Power.

7. Reviewing our past in the company of other Last Thirders has shown us that our earlier life goals no longer suffice.

8. Through reading, discussion, and reflection, we have humbly attempted to discover and cultivate those higher values that are essential to our new life.

9. Having thus gained a clearer perspective on life's major phases, we have steadfastly sought the wisdom it is the business of life's later years to acquire and preserve.

10. These steps have brought an awareness of cosmic dimensions we had not hitherto explored and have led us into the realm of deep spiritual experience.

11. Though aware that the workaday world undervalues spiritual wisdom, we offer what we have of it when asked.

12. As our special responsibility, and as opportunity offers, we carry to others in the final third of life the heartening word that seniority can be joyous.

Thus have we, whom the world would cast off as being of no further use to it, recovered from our confusion, regained the spiritual initiative, and begun to pour into the world as much as we can of the thing it needs most—wisdom.

Our road is not always smooth, and we are not above using simple catch phrases, slogans, prayers, and proverbs to see us through moments of unusual stress. These are among our favorites: First things first, Live and let live, Think, It takes all kinds, One day at a time, The time is now. We frequently use these prayers: "O God, give me the serenity to accept what cannot be changed—Give me the courage to change what can be changed—And the wisdom to know the one from the other" and "God help me seek to understand rather than to be understood, to love rather than to be loved, to comfort rather than to be comforted, to serve rather than to be served."

We keep fresh in memory those paragraphs from our reading that have seemed to us to carry special meaning for those passing into the last third of life— especially those passages which illuminate our view into the far future. This, from Dr. Jung, is a favorite: An aim of education "is to transform a human being into a new—a future—man, and to allow the old forms of life to die away." It is to change

into that other, foreign, "also-I" [and let] the earlier ego vanish into the past. . . . It is particularly fatal for such people [in the later part of life] to look backward. . . . This is why all great religions hold the promise of a life beyond; it makes it possible for mortal man to live the second half of life with as much perseverance and aim as the first.[3]

And this, from the book *Unknown But Known:*

A general emancipation from the searing grip of the most fearsome of all dreads—the fear of death—would free tremendous human energies for the creative tasks of life. And there is no *rational* reason for delaying any longer a general enjoyment of this immeasurable benefit. A hundred years of careful research has established the essential fact of survival to the satisfaction of all who approach the evidence with a free mind. Three thousand years of demonstration by prophets, saints and heroes has suggested the capacity for expanded living that results when a human being casts aside his fear of death. There is no longer any rational reason to consider biological death a final end, or to fear it.[4]

As a result of all we have reported in this book, we have experienced a new, continuing, and increasing joy and creativity. In gratitude we share it when and as we can. This sharing we call Condition Twelve: "As our special responsibility, and as opportunity offers, we carry to others in the final third of life the heartening word that seniority can be joyous." If you care to join us, or if you'd like to start a Last Third of Life Club in your own community, write to us.

APPENDIX I

"It Leaves Me with the Feeling That I Would Not Be Afraid to Die"

A Review of *Deathbed Observations by Physicians and Nurses* by Dr. Karlis Osis (New York: Parapsychology Foundation, Division of Research, 1961).

Not long ago one of our members was asked to give a talk on the modern attitude toward the personal, subjective experience of dying. To advertise this event, the sponsoring group had a poster prepared. It placarded the announcement in white letters—against a background of a large, somber, grim, black *coffin!*

Our colleague good-naturedly protested. "But it's not *like* that," he said. "Death may be a somber occasion for those left behind; if the departed was well beloved, they'll miss him. But all the modern evidence suggests that for the one who makes the actual trip, the occasion is much more likely to be one not of blackness but of color, joy, and beauty."

Due to the activities of our resourceful and indefatigable psychic researchers, the matter has been pretty well taken out of the realm of opinion and moved over into the area of fact. Three large-scale studies of moment-of-death experience have been made in the twentieth century—one in England, two in the United States. All agree that the experience of dying is far more likely to be pleasant, or even ecstatic, than it is to be unpleasant.

This corroborates the experience of a great many of us who had "close calls" or who know people who have. The eminent Swiss psychiatrist Carl Jung, who has been quoted elsewhere in this book, had a particularly vivid experience of this kind—and a fairly typical one. In 1944, when Jung was sixty-nine years old, he suffered a severe heart attack and lay in coma, between life and death, for three weeks. During this period he had the following experience, here described in his own words on page 289 of his 1961 autobiography *Memories, Dreams, Reflections* (Random House) :

I found myself in an utterly transformed state, in an ecstacy. I was floating in space a thousand miles above the earth, which I could clearly see below me. I felt safe in the womb of the universe, with a happiness that cannot be described. Soon I saw a gigantic stone, a huge asteroid, also floating in space. Inside it was a splendid, illuminated temple, and there—I felt with a great certainty—I was about to meet those people to whom I really belonged.

Then a messenger arrived. I was ordered back to earth to finish the work that was expected of me. I was profoundly disappointed. Earth life seemed to me a prison. I had been glad to shed it all, and felt a violent resistance to returning.

The latest and most extensive of the three major twentieth-century studies of hour-of-death experiences was conducted by Dr. Karlis Osis, Director of Research at the Parapsychology Foundation in New York. This research was undertaken in 1961 and covered 35,000 cases. Of these, more than 3,500 patients were fully conscious and mentally alert at the moment of death. The observers were all doctors and nurses in American hospitals—trained persons long practiced in carefully observing and accurately reporting the mental and physical states of human beings. Osis' findings confirm in a startling way the *near*-death experiences so often reported in ordinary experience. Here are some excerpts from the Osis report:

The doctors and nurses in our sample reported that *fear* is *not* the dominant emotion in dying patients. On the contrary, a large number of patients are said to be *elated* at the hour of death. This strengthens the evidence of previous findings.

Many spontaneous comments were made by our respondents. A general practitioner commented that such observations had changed his philosophy: "A peaceful, happy expression comes over the patient," he said. "It leaves me with a feeling that I would not be afraid to die."

One doctor reported a near-death experience of his own: his near-drowning brought him to such a beautiful state of consciousness that he was unhappy at being rescued. This was true also of *patients* who had been close to death but were brought back. Characteristic responses were: "Why did you bring me back, doctor? It was so nice there," or, "I want to go back, let me go back." The experience can be so gratifying that after them many patients have a strong wish to die. Except for the characteristic "voice commanding them to return," there seems to be no essential difference between terminal and non-terminal experiences in the early phases . . . the predominant emotions at death's door were calmness, peace and exaltation. . . .

The predominance of visions of persons known to have died seems to be a very real characteristic of terminal cases. It may very well be that this type of experience goes beyond the individual himself, and indicates an external activity involving post-mortem existence of the dead.

In other branches of psychical research it has been found that the experience of meeting one who has already made the death transition is the first knowledge the dying person has of what is actually happening to him. In this situation, there is sometimes an awareness of facts that could not possibly have come to the person by the usual earth channels. The Osis report makes special mention of such a case. For many weeks a woman patient lay critically ill in a hospital. During this period her sister—named Vida—fell ill and died. Because of the patient's own extremely precarious condition, this news was kept from her. The woman's last moments are described in the Osis report as follows:

As the woman's death approached she said, "It is all so dark, I cannot see." A moment later her face brightened and she exclaimed: "Oh, it is so lovely and bright; you can't see as I can." A little later: "I can see father" (her father was long dead). Then, with a puzzled expression: "He has Vida with him. Vida is with him!" A moment later she died.

It would appear from the accumulating evidence of this kind that we may reasonably expect three things when we die: (1) the experience of an indescribably beautiful setting, (2) the friendly meeting with an acquaintance who has gone ahead of us, and (3) a strong preference for what lies in the future over what lies in the past.

APPENDIX II

"It Is Heartbreaking Even to Try to Write of It"

A Review of *The Life Beyond Death* by Arthur Ford (New York: G. P. Putnam's Sons, 1971).

The American Christian clergy, as well as American Christian laymen—to say nothing of people having no religious convictions of any kind!—are sharply divided on the matter of how seriously one should take psychic phenomena and the findings of psychical researchers. Spiritual Frontiers Fellowship, a nationwide psychic-education fellowship whose founding members included the celebrated trance medium Arthur Ford and some very distinguished Christian clergymen, encourages psychic research and widely disseminates information concerning psychical happenings and processes. And, of course, equally distinguished Christian clergymen could be found who would roundly denounce the whole business.

The Last Third Club, with its firm position of respecting the individual member's personal life experience in all things, takes no official position in the matter. We simply report that a number of our members have found a particular passage of the book now under review to be of special interest—and provocative of unending conversation. This is the automatic writing purporting to be the report of Frederic W. H. Myers on the structure, conditions, and experiences of the life beyond death.

Myers was born in 1843 and raised in the Anglican Christian tradition. He became a lecturer in classics at Cambridge and, as an intellectual, felt the full impact of the militant materialistic atheism which was the intellectual vogue of his time. The general assault on religion, on spirit, and particularly on metaphysics had a profound impact on the sensitive Myers. The attack on the Resurrection, and with it the possibility of a life beyond death, particularly concerned him. Was there really a life in spirit, continuing after one's earthly demise? Myers had to *know;* his entire religious faith was at stake.

So he—together with the philosopher Henry Sidgwick and the psychologist Edmund Gurney (both of them fellow members of the Cambridge faculty) and other distinguished Englishmen—formed the Society for Psychical Research in order to find out. The work of this society began in 1882. Its original aims were two: to research the phenomenon of telepathy and to investigate the claims of mediums that they could sometimes put one in touch with people presumed dead but who lived on in spirit.

A great many of these mediums, it turned out, were fraudulent. Fraud was easy to expose, and a far more difficult problem—the problem of telepathy (also called "mind-reading," "thought-reading," and "mental radio")—soon took over Myers' attention. Not all the mediums, the researchers discovered, were swindlers. However, Myers strongly suspected that some of the material taken to be spirit communication was actually drawn telepathically from living minds; it was the unconscious content of the minds of persons alive and on the earth.

But spirit communication, if real, would itself be a form of telepathy. How could one tell the difference between spirit telepathy and earth telepathy? It was an extremely knotty problem, and Myers set out to solve it. He finally did—but not until after his death.

Myers died in 1901. His great two-volume treatise

called *Human Personality and Its Survival of Bodily Death*—the basic work underpinning all modern survival research—was published in 1903. By 1906, all three founders of the SPR—Myers, Sidgwick, and Gurney—were dead. In that year there began that astonishing series of spirit communications known as the "Cross-Correspondences." Providing apparently irrefutable evidence of a life beyond death, and disposing once and for all of the telepathy problems, these consistent communications constitute the most imposing body of evidence known to survival research.

The messages continued for thirty-two years, from 1906 to 1938. They were transmitted in "automatic writing"—mediumistic writing while in trance or semitrance—by five different mediums, none of them known to any of the others. The total correspondence fills 3,000 pages of the *Proceedings of the SPR*. The messages were signed by Myers, Sidgwick, and Gurney and were so artfully contrived that they could have been sent *only* by the signer. The individual messages were arranged so they made no sense by themselves, thus ruling out any possibility of earth telepathy, and they went on for so long that no combination of the participating earth people could have arranged them. Yet when all the "senseless" messages were pieced together according to directions—something made possible by the "spirit-message clearinghouse" system the SPR maintained at the time—the total communication had a beautiful and crystal-clear pattern.

When this gigantic work "from the other side" was well in hand, the communications signed "Myers" began the task of describing to earth minds the kind of life they might expect to lead after death. For this work "Myers" selected a young nonprofessional medium, Miss Geraldine Cummins of Cork, daughter of a professor and gifted in automatic writing. In the seven years between 1924 and 1931, several hundred pages on the life beyond death were transmitted through Miss Cummins.

The communications describe the afterlife as consisting of seven "planes." Each plane carries the soul a step closer to the Divine Being, the Radiant Source, the Center from which emanates all Creation—God. Each plane is separated from the next higher by a death-and-rebirth experience. During each such transition, one sheds the grosser structures of the past and enters new dimensions of subtlety, intensity, and range.

These are the seven planes:

Stage One is the earth plane—the level on which we now find ourselves. Stage Two is "The Corridor Immediately After Death." This stage is fairly brief. Its chief characteristic is the "Long Trip Down Memory Lane." One's entire earth experience is reviewed in a leisurely, sleepy, restful way. People who have had narrow escapes from death often report a kind of newsreel of their lives flashing instantaneously before them. This might well be the beginning of the "Stage Two Review." It is followed by a stretch of rest and readjustment.

Stage Three, named by Myers "The Plane of Illusion," is the first stable and enduring plane after death. This is the plane from which most mediumistic messages reach earth people. Here one is met, shown around, and made to feel at home by earthside friends who have gone before. Here one very gradually sheds the illusions of earth existence—clinging, however, to enough of them so that the change will not be traumatic. One has clothing, houses, friends as of yore. The terrain features trees, foliage, mountains, and rivers. There are alternate periods of light and dark, more or less resembling our day and night. Sun and stars are sometimes visible, but everything is self-luminous rather than lighted from outside itself. One sleeps now and then but soon ceases to crave food. Energy is derived directly from a radiant environment with no need to be passed through a digestive system. Communication is direct mind-to-mind by telepathic images; this system eliminates the need for words and language.

Movement from one scene to another is accomplished by thought. Since many of the needs of living can be simply *imagined* into existence, there is no need for money or commerce. Success or failure is measured not in material gain or loss but in spiritual development or regression. Once one has made his adjustment to the new plane, he takes on two responsibilities: He is expected to meet and help newcomers as he was met and helped.

Sooner or later one must decide whether to go back to earth—"reincarnate"—or strive for the next higher level of consciousness. Curious, adventurous, intelligent, ethically mature souls invariably press on. People too firmly attached to earth ways go back—become a fetus again, then a baby, and go through the whole earth business all over again, perhaps to do better this time in terms of spiritual growth. Many find themselves so content on The Plane of Illusion that they imagine it to be the ultimate heaven and remain there for centuries. But they must in the end make up their minds—onward or backward.

Stage Four Myers calls "The Plane of Color," also known as "Eidos." Myers says he was living on this plane at the time of writing, twenty-five years after his earth death. On the Fourth Plane one leaves behind the last vestiges of earth thinking. Myers is very insistent on this "breaking of the image," as he calls it. He writes: "One must leave behind all rigid intellectual structures and dogmas, whether they be scientific, religious or philosophical." On Plane Four

Myers is beginning to have trouble finding words to describe what he is experiencing. He writes: "It is impossible for an earth-being to imagine the infinite variety of new sounds, colors and feelings known to us here." Though indescribable joy is experienced, one is not yet finished with trouble and woe: "The soul must struggle and labor, know sorrow but not earth-sorrow, ecstacy but not earth-ecstacy. Not only love, truth and beauty are present, but also hostility, hate and anger. The main work here is further understanding of how mind controls energy and life-force, from which all *outward* appearances emerge."

The Fifth Plane is The Plane of Flame, also known as "Helios." Here one acquires a body of flame. One may then tour the entire stellar universe without being harmed by its temperatures and turbulence. The Sixth Plane is The Plane of Light. Persons at this level, Myers says, are matured spirits: "They have consciously lived through all the aspects of the Divine Creation. They have won the incalculable secret wisdom. They have fulfilled the ultimate purpose of the evolution of consciousness." In the Seventh and final plane one enters into full partnership with God. This, Myers confesses, is still far beyond the reach of his comprehension. He simply says, "It is heartbreaking even to try to write of it."

Let us repeat: the inclusion of this review does not constitute endorsement of Myers' metaphysics by The Last Third Club. The club does not endorse anything— it is simply a program of personal growth toward a specific objective. This, however, we can pretty much guarantee—the "Myers message" can infallibly be counted on to produce some lively and mind-stretching conversation!

APPENDIX III

The Stages of Life

A Review of *Modern Man in Search of a Soul* by Carl G. Jung (New York: Harcourt, Brace & World, 1933; Harvest Book edition, n.d.).

Though anyone would find nourishing food for thought in reading *all* of this little classic, the passage of greatest value to members of The Last Third Club—and the exclusive topic of the present review—is chapter 5, to which Jung has given the title, "The Stages of Life."

In this passage Jung divides life into four parts: (1) childhood, (2) youth, (3) "reversal at noon," and (4) the later years. Living by instinct, as one does in childhood, is living by nature and presents few conscious problems, since there is so little consciousness. Problems, in the adult sense of the word, are first encountered in Phase Two—youth—with the emergence of sexual life in puberty.

It is through encountering and dealing with problems, Jung says, that we accomplish the central purpose of human life, which is the evolution of our souls to even higher levels of consciousness. "Youth" is defined as the period from just after puberty to just after the thirty-fifth year. Transition from each stage to the next is accompanied by a sequence of problems involving "duality"—a conflict between a desire to be one's age and a residual desire to cling to the pleasures of the preceding age. Thus youth tends to hold on to aspects of childish behavior, and someone in the second half of life often shows a reluctance to let go the pleasures of youth.

In no case, however, can one maintain the behavior patterns of an earlier phase of life without damage to one's soul. The conflict cannot be escaped. The problems it engenders must be faced and coped with on the level of one's true chronological age. Failure to do so means sacrifice of one's life opportunity to grow in character, mind, and spirit.

Problems, Jung maintains, are tragically misunderstood by the popular mind, which would like to avoid them. But avoidance of problems means avoidance of the central meaning of life. Problems are opportunities for growth. They force the mind and spirit into ever wider and deeper ranges of awareness, which is true development of spirit. One may think of it, he says, as a struggle between nature and culture. Nature is primitive, narrow, obsessed only with its own ends, basically unconscious and automatic, totally oblivious to the requirements of individual, social, and cultural development. Such values of culture and the further evolution of consciousness are beyond the reach of nature. They are attained only by conscious effort exerted during the second half of life.

During the period of "youth," not much is accomplished in this direction. Youth finds its social being in limiting itself "to the attainable" and finding its way through its pressing problems by achievement within the norms of the society. The price paid is the temporary abandonment of all other possibilities, including "that wider consciousness to which we give the name of culture."

Before the struggles of youth have appreciably diminished, one is overtaken by the formidable complexities of the "reversal" at the "noon" of life. Statistics show an increase in cases of mental depression in men of about the age of forty, while in women such difficulties generally begin a few years earlier. Vast changes are under way, not only in mind and spirit but even in body and mannerisms. Men tend toward a rather feminine bodily roundness and sometimes a new gentleness, while women may show such presumably masculine traits as deeper voices, harder features, and a liking to manage and command. One tends to be thrown into confusion. Shall one try to fake the old ways of childhood and youth—against such formidable competition and at the price of making a fool of oneself? The values of the first half of life are clearly fading, but where are the values of the second half? When, where, and how do they begin to emerge? It is here that Jung delivers himself of his famous remark that schools to prepare one for the second half of life are as urgently needed as are schools to prepare one for the first. "Whoever carries over into the afternoon [of life] the law of the morning—that is, the aims of nature—must pay for so doing," he concludes, "with damage to his soul."

Jung insists that man would not have been allotted this long stretch of later years unless it had a specific and important meaning. What, then, *is* this meaning, and how may one fulfill it? He refuses to say categorically, but he drops some interesting hints. "Our religions," he writes, "were always such schools in the past, but how many . . . of us older persons have really been brought up in such a school and prepared for the second half of life, for old age, death and eternity?"

He adds:

It is particularly fatal for such people [on the threshold of old age] to look backward. For them a prospect and a goal in the future are indispensable. This is why all great religions hold the promise of a life beyond; it makes it possible for mortal man to live the second half of life with as much perseverance and aim as the first. . . . I have observed [as a physician] . . . that it is better to go forwards with the stream of time than backwards against it.

... It is hygienic ... to discover in death a goal towards which one can strive; and that shrinking away from it is something unhealthy and abnormal which robs the second half of life of its purpose. . . . When I live in a house which I know will fall about my head within the next two weeks, all my vital functions will be impaired by this thought; but if on the contrary I feel myself to be safe, I can dwell there in a normal and comfortable way. From the standpoint of psychotherapy it would therefore be desirable to think of death as only a transition. . . .

He remarks in a later passage that this recommendation does not necessarily imply adherence to any institutionalized faith or religious organization. Such creed or membership, he says, "has nothing whatever" to do with it. It is the confident belief that counts.

But there is much more to these later years, Dr. Jung remarks, than just preparing creatively to die. "Could by any chance culture be the meaning and purpose of the second half of life?" Here he points out that the older people of the early tribes were always the guardians of the cultural heritage of the people—the standards, values, mysteries, and laws. Then he asks, as if in direct challenge to all of us to get busy on the matter, "How does the matter stand with us? Where is the wisdom of our old people— where are their precious secrets and their visions? . . . Only a very few people are artists in life; . . . the art of life is the most distinguished and rarest of all the arts."

In this passage it is quite clear that when he uses the word "culture" he does not use it in the sense of an accumulation of academic knowledge. Culture is rather that special sense, gathered in the relative quiet of the later years and available alike to educated savant and unlettered peasant, that he has called "the most distinguished and rarest of all the arts"—the art of life.

APPENDIX IV

The State of One's Health:
Margins of Mystery

A Review of *The Light That Heals: A Modern Testimony of Spiritual Healing* (Privately printed, 1970, available through Phenix Club Secretary, Box 25, Guilford, Connecticut 06437.)

"There's one thing you notice about being older," one of our members recently remarked. "You're not as robust as you used to be." Trite? Yes. A Truism? For certain. Yet it's a truism we of the later years have to face and cope with. Some of our parts are beginning to wear out. Every now and then one of them has to be repaired or, if it's too far gone, taken out and thrown away. Sickness or the threat of it seems to be a bigger part of our lives than it used to be.

This presents us with a personal problem of no small size. We obstinately refuse to become hypochondriacs, impairing our usefulness to others by becoming obsessed with our symptoms and forever wailing about our health. We have known all along that these bodies would some day wear out, either piecemeal or all at once, and that we would die. We are no longer afraid of dying; that is not the problem.

The problem is how to handle the health business, emotionally speaking, until we *do* make The Big Trip. We are sometimes faced with hard decisions that can't be ducked. For example: one of our members had some kidney trouble. Doctor A, a surgeon, said, "Let's take the kidney out and be rid of both the kidney and the trouble." Doctor B, equally competent, said "A's just a natural-born cutter—he'd cut your throat if you gave him the chance. Leave the kidney where it is and let's help it get well." The patient, of course, is unschooled in the complex specializations of materialistic medicine. Yet *he*—and *only* he—must decide. What shall he do? What shall he say?

To complicate matters further, there is the thought-provoking and well-substantiated statistic that two thirds of the general run of medical complaints get well by themselves. Though this is based on general-population experience and probably does not apply to our age group, it nonetheless gives one pause. To deepen one's perplexity still further, word comes to us from time to time of spontaneous healing of a most startling kind, sometimes associated with psychological, psychic, or religious procedures. What should one do? How does one plot one's course in this kind of a fog? These are the questions to which the little book here under review addresses itself.

The Light That Heals is compiled from the minutes of a conference of representatives of all the healing arts, held at Wainright House in Rye, N.Y. "Never in the history of healing," says the book's Introduction,

has there been assembled in a single conference such a diversity of healing gifts and methods. The purpose was to exchange information by which the spiritual principles underlying restoration of physical, mental, and spiritual health might better be understood. Men of objective science mingled with faith-healers; Anglican high-churchmen chatted with trance-mediums; Protestant clergymen chatted with a Hindu Swami. Psychiatrists and specially qualified nurses traded experiences with hospital chaplains.

There were fifty-two conferees, representing three countries and eleven U.S. states. There were seven medical doctors, seven psychiatrists, two university professors of medicine, twenty clergymen representing five major denominations (and, as chaplains, two world-renowned hospitals), and ten qualified laymen.

The most dramatic aspect of the conference was the wide variety of healings reported—and the heartbreaking failures. The chaplain of a large New York hospital cited two contrasting cases from the many in his experience. In Case One, a child of four fell from a fifth-story window; the doctors found no pulse and no hope. Prayers were said and the child recovered. In Case Two a child fell from a fourth-floor window and was given up under circumstances strikingly similar to Case One. Prayers were said and the child died.

As for the success or failure of spiritual healing, a medical-school professor said that, in adult cases, the important thing was not alone what the healers did but what the attitude of the patient was. Are people prepared and receptive, or doubtful and negative? In one instance there was a large-scale hay-fever test in which half the patients were injected with a ragweed agent known to have therapeutic effect and half were injected with plain water. The doctors giving the injections did not know which material they were using. Half the patients receiving the plain water were relieved of their hay fever. A common denominator in all healings, said the professor, was the patient's faith in what was going on.

A famous British authority expressed strong opposition to methods that place the burden of healing entirely on the patient's faith. He cited a much-publicized healer he thought was doing much damage. If a healing took place the healer took the credit; if not, the patient was blamed for having too little faith. It was a case of "heads I win, tails you lose." Failures should be accepted, he said, as an indication that the right way to cooperate with God for the occasion had not yet been found. Other conferees, commenting on the same problem, had a variety of opinions: "The favorable conditions for healing are positive expectancy, open-mindedness, and accord; I have seen amazing things happen under these conditions." Another authority deplored the amount of negative, despairing thinking there was in the world, almost having the effect of a *wish* for illness: "the big job is to turn off the faucet that's drenching the world with sickness, instead of just mopping up after it. Many sick people seem *deliberately* to separate themselves from influences that could be beneficial to them."

Pressing too hard for a healing without a corresponding effort toward inner change and growth was warned against by several authorities: "Some people want to be healed without being changed—a thing that is often a patent impossibility, since the illness itself is being caused by faulty attitudes that need changing." And: "Willingness to surrender is *so* important; a readiness to let the healing force come in and do anything it wanted to." And: "The healing principles, in my opinion, are these: transferring confidence from oneself to a greater power, receiving forgiveness and strength, not allowing the mind to be empty, and filling it with constructive thoughts and useful activity." And: "The negative emotions—anger, resentment, fear, hate, dread—if long-sustained, can and do produce destructive bodily changes. The positive emotions of love, forgiveness, trust, and sympathetic understanding can change the body back to health again."

Despite the mysteries and uncertainties, many spectacular healings have occurred under conditions where conclusive verification was possible. A patient was sent to a hospital to undergo an operation for a tumor which might have been malignant. The patient called the church and was given a sacrament in the hospital.

140

When the surgeon arrived for preoperational procedures, he found the x-rays showed no tumor in the place where previously there had been one. A Hindu swami commented that religious healing was not limited to the Western religious traditions. He recalled seeing a man with a hopeless case of tuberculosis instantly healed when spoken to by a priest who was an advanced soul. Commenting on the possibility of demon possession, he averred that such cases undoubtedly exist, that no experienced observer who has seen such a case could mistake it for anything else, and that the demon, in the East as in the West, can be exorcised by appropriate and spiritually competent religious procedures. A British authority supported him on these points.

Many cases bore out the connection between healing and attitude change. A psychiatrist cited a case where a woman developed cancer of the breast and was operated on. Psychotherapy was then begun. At this time there was also a lung cancer. As a reconciliation progressed between the patient and her daughter, the lung healed. Another conferee mentioned the case of a young Irish writer with mental despair coupled physically with lung hemorrhage. Over a period of years he made a spiritual journey from violent love-hate conflicts to radiant friendliness—and resulting confident health.

The healing power of prayer was discussed at length, and many well-witnessed case histories were cited. Dr. Leslie Weatherhead, author of the pace-setting book *Psychiatry, Religion and Healing* (Abingdon Press), said he had seen an inoperable cancer patient, turned away by the surgeons, healed by prayer. Yet he did not think that prayer was always a more relevant way of cooperating with God than physical surgery or the sometimes even more effective mental surgery of psychotherapy. "Prayer," he said, "is *valuable* in every situation but not necessarily *curative* in every situation."

There was an abundance of testimony from conference members on prayer-based or sacrament-based healing. Such cases—some of them validated by official medical documentation—included cancer, heart disease, tuberculosis, asthma, and violent mental illness healed at a distance. Temporary and partial healings, followed by relapse, were also noted. In India, there was a case of brain cancer causing blindness. Prayer was offered. X-rays showed that the cancer had then receded; sight returned to one eye. For six months the patient was tremendously effective in religious work— then he died of the cancer. (The question naturally arises: Was he granted the extra months to finish necessary work?) A kidney complaint was healed by a simple touch of a healer's hand. Prayer groups have an impressive record. One patient, dying of ptomaine poisoning, said, "I suddenly felt fire in my veins—and I was well! I later learned that a chain of prayer groups all across the city had been praying for me at that moment." A child with a burst appendix, hundreds of miles from the nearest medical aid, was prayed for by her parents and recovered.

Some spiritual healings take months or even years; others are instantaneous. A New Jersey minister told of a brain-injury case. As a result of a railroad wreck, one of his young parishioners lay unconscious in the hospital for a week. A brain surgeon was scheduled to operate on Monday morning. At the Sunday worship service the day before, the preacher felt strongly moved to change his usual formal general prayer to a prayer he improvised especially for his injured parishioner. He knew the exact time, because he believed in running punctual services and had noted the clock when he began the new prayer. At that exact moment, nurses in the hospital reported that the patient regained consciousness. The surgeon, arriving the next morning, testified that the patient was fully recovered and canceled the operation. ";How wonderful it would be," one conferee commented, "if in every community, doctors asked ministers and their congregations, 'May I have the benefit of your prayers in helping with some of my more difficult healings?' "

One of the high points of the conference was the testimony concerning the disease known as alcoholism, which snatches so many thousands each year from the threshold of the last third of life. A cofounder of Alcoholics Anonymous described the founding of this now-worldwide movement and his early experiences in it. A New York businessman he called Roland went to Carl Jung to be cured of his alcoholism. The great psychiatrist told Roland his case was beyond the reach of the usual methods; only a transforming religious experience could save him. Such experiences could never be guaranteed, but Roland could, if he chose, start off by exposing himself to some religious ideas and practices. Roland chose a popular religious movement of the time called the Oxford Group. There he met another alcoholic, Ebbie, and together, within the influence of the group, they stayed sober. Ebbie was a former drinking friend of the speaker. Ebbie called and found the speaker at his kitchen table with a bottle of gin, drunk. At this time, the summer of 1934, the speaker's situation was desperate and he knew it. Doctors had told his wife he'd go mad and die if he kept up his drinking much longer. Impressed by Ebbie's happy sobriety, he asked about the rules for obtaining it and was told: be honest with yourself, talk out your situation with a right-thinking friend, make restitution for wrongs you have done, pray, do a little giving without reward. The speaker was deeply moved—and got drunk again. He was taken to a hospital and placed under the care of Dr. W. D.

143

Silkworth. In the hospital the speaker was seized by an overwhelming depression. Throwing himself on his knees he cried in utter abandonment, "If there is a God let Him show Himself!" An ecstasy followed. After it, the speaker asked Dr. Silkworth whether he'd been hallucinating. Dr. Silkworth said he'd read about such experiences in William James's *Varieties of Religious Experience* but had never before seen an instance of it. He advised the speaker to believe in it and follow where it led. From the moment of the experience, the obsession to drink was expelled, and it never returned. The speaker then set out to pass the word on to other alcoholics—and thus Alcoholics Anonymous was born.

At the closing session Dr. Weatherhead addressed himself to that baffling question: What about those who pray and still remain unhealed? As a minister, he reminded the conference that healing was not the only freight carried by religion. Jesus himself endured death by violence and some of his apostles suffered disease. He did not advise pressing too hard for immediate healing, or regarding it as the sole or even the major aim of maintaining a spiritual philosophy. Frequently while in his church, he said, he wore a cross given to him by a girl who later died of an incurable condition after having been to Lourdes, where one-hundredth of one percent of patients are pronounced healed. "Take this," she had said on giving it to him, "It taught me not to mind, in trust of God, whether you get better or not."

On this theme Dr. Weatherhead commented:

There can be superb faith without healing, and superb healing without faith. Jesus always put his teaching first, and frequently soft-pedaled his healing. Harm can be done by healing the patient and leaving him no wiser. The record says Jesus healed not everybody but "many."

Failures in our time must be accepted with the understanding that the important thing is not healing but co-operation with God. It seems almost as if God were saying, "I can get you where I want you to be as effectively in sickness as in health." In postponed healings we must see as though through bi-focal glasses—the long-distance part focused on recovery, the bottom half on acceptance: "I willingly take this thing."

A New York psychiatrist spoke in support of this point of view. He cited a man dying of Parkinson's disease who had accepted his affliction not only as part of his later life but as a meaningful end to it. At the end the man said, "Now I know what religious people mean when they speak of being 'at peace with God.'"

What has this little book to do with living out the Twelve Conditions of The Last Third Club? By the time we have reached the last third of life we have known many illnesses and many recoveries—most of them routine, some mysterious or even spectacular. The testimony of *The Light That Heals* gives a great variety of evidence on the specific workings of the healing spirit and to that extent adds to our wisdom, hence to our potential for usefulness. As for ourselves, we quite naturally want favorable health right to the end. We know, however, that no matter how many of our sicknesses are healed there will come that last one which will not. We do not fear it. It is the ticket to our Big Trip. We can say, when the time comes, "I willingly take this thing." We can say, "I know the meaning of being at peace with God."

APPENDIX V

Harry's Case

Call me Harry—I'm one of the original Last Third-
clubbers, and we use only first names as an aid to
candor. At meetings it's our custom to have somebody
lead off with a brief account of his experience with the
Last Third Club—before, first months, and now. I've
been asked to tell what I do on these occasions, as a
possible example for people who may want to start
a local Last Third Club or lead one of its meetings.
What I do is very simple: I just tell my story. Since
I sometimes talk better than I write, this may not be
very good, but I'll do what I can.

We believe we've found something valuable, and
we've learned that we can't keep it unless we give it
away. The leader appointed for a particular meeting
tells his story, then invites other members to comment
from their own experience. Soon a lively discussion is
under way. Thus, new experience is fed into the group,
questions find answers, problems get solved, friend-
ships based on mutual understanding develop, and
the Last Third idea spreads.

About my own case. I was muddling through somehow until I was sixty. Then it really hit me—"it"
being whatever you want to call it; preretirement syndrome, male menopause, empty-nest blues, geriatric
depression, gerontology melanchology, or whatever. I
had been hit by things before, of course; you don't
get to be sixty without having known a few knocks.

But every problem I'd had before carried the possibility of solution. There was something I could *do*
about it, if only I could find out what. This new thing
had what seemed to be an absolute *dead-endedness*
about it that got me down. What did I have to look

forward to but aging, old age, terminal illness, and death—all things I had rigorously avoided giving any thought to all my life on grounds that they were negative and depressing. Now, despite liberal applications of such commonly recommended remedies as travel, hobbies, social contacts, and the like, I couldn't think of anything else! Nor could I find any way to set my mind at ease on these matters. I lived in almost intolerable anxiety.

My presixty life had been one containing some sharp ups and downs, but on the whole I suppose it could be regarded, by the yardstick of our society's usual standards, as moderately successful. As a young man I had, after a brief stretch of post-college poverty, really sky-rocketing success. At thirty-five I was in top command of a continent-wide enterprise. I had my own airplane and flew it myself to wherever I felt like going. I had a family coming along, many friends, and wide opportunity for new experience and self-development. I so thoroughly blew all this in booze and self-indulgence that by the time I was forty I was divorced, out of a job, and broke. I got rid of the booze, started over with a new wife and a new profession, and slowly made my way back. Things came along nicely enough so that by the time I was sixty I "had it made" again rather comfortably. Then what was the matter? Why this gnawing, unrelenting, almost continuous depression?

One thing was health. Before I was sixty I had never been in a hospital except to visit friends. Then, in a stretch of twenty months, I had two long bouts of major surgery. Even I could be seriously sick! It was, to me, a profoundly unsettling discovery.

At about this time, two old friends of mine, also go-getter types and also long accustomed to near-perfect health, also became acquainted with serious illness—one had a heart attack, the other a stroke.

These close approaches of death loosened our tongues about the previously taboo subjects of aging, death, and a possible beyond. Before that it had been our habit to brush aside such matters with a hollow heartiness and some breezy bragging.

Fortunately, all three of us recovered. But the shocking discovery that we were mortals caused us to take stock. It happened that we all were readers. We began to read up on what had been bugging us—our inexorable aging and approaching death. Now we talked freely, not only about what we thought and felt but also about what we had read. Our depressions (my two friends had them too!) began to lift. They were replaced by a whole new world-outlook; this was the beginning of the Last Third Club. We didn't have a name for it then, but we *had* hit on its basic principle: if you can talk out a thing with other intelligent people who are creatively trying to cope with the same set of problems, your depression will lift and you will begin to resume your growth toward wisdom and maturity.

During my depressions I became known to family and friends as a once-genial man who was turning into an old grouch. To me (and I guess to herself, though she'd better tell that part) my wife was a particular problem. I think she was having a touch of empty-nest syndrome; the children had grown up and left. I know she was struggling through late menopause, and on top of that she had employment problems: she wanted to work but couldn't find a job. So, for the first time since our marriage, things around home were somewhat less than pleasant. I continued talking with my old friends—one of them regularly once a week, the other when we could manage. Both of them, now that they had begun verbalizing on life-and-death topics, reported that they had found other aging men and women ready to talk frankly. Our circle slowly began to grow.

As we continued to compare notes, we found that there was more to it than just a regular talking-it-out. We found, in fact, as our searching went on and our experience widened, that there were *twelve main points*, each one in its own time pivotal to the success of the whole later-life enterprise. These finally became refined into what we now call our Twelve Conditions. One of our founders signed up for a course in meditation and came back with a glowing report. I followed suit. Thereafter, solitary meditation became a daily habit for both of us. When the time came to formulate our experience this became Condition Six: "Through regular morning and evening meditations, we are finding ourselves more and more in harmony with this transcendent Power." This was the real turning point of my Last Third Club experience.

The grouchiness subsided and the depression relented. Things were going better, and for quite a while I was unable to say exactly why. Then, slowly, I began to realize that somehow I had tapped an inner source of strength and enlightenment. I became aware of the vast differences between inner truth and external appearance. All my life I had been forced to focus on externals; to focus on anything else was regarded as idle daydreaming. But the externals, when applied to the stretch of life that now lay ahead of me—aging, old age, a probable terminal illness, death and a possible world beyond—left me absolutely nothing. In its purely outward aspects, this passage of life seemed to offer mainly progressing ugliness, weakness, worry, fear, pain, grief, stupidity, querulousness, confinement, depression, and quarrelsomeness.

But the inner landscape, once it was really discovered and lived in, was aglow with beauty, strength, serenity, love, joy, intelligence, creativity, freedom, happiness, and harmony. I became keenly aware that my body was only an external view of the activity of my spirit as it assembled and manipulated such molecules as it had temporary need of. I began to see clearly that *I was not my body.* I came to think of earth-life as a great, bounteously bearing fruit tree, and of each of us as a piece of ripening fruit. We flower, grow, and ripen, and when fully ripe, drop from the tree, take root in fresh soil, and begin to grow in new life. In daily meditation we turn away from externals toward our inner light, and there in the depths of the soul we experience the divine. To know the divine means to know oneself in relation to the cosmos, to experience the ascending force of life in all things.

The view from cosmic consciousness is clearer. One can see that the presumed terrors of aging, old age, terminal illness, and transition to another consciousness are all temporary things. They come, have their moment, and go, just as the crises of our earlier earth-life came and passed. But the glory of cosmic creative life goes on, and we believe we can go on with it if we choose to. Aging, I observed not very originally, takes place one day at a time. So does growth in maturity. My roadblock had been made up of a lifetime of imprint and conditioning in externals. Its removal through extinction of negative conditioning by massed trials was slow. But it was sure, and as it progressed I was able to forge ahead with the other Conditions toward realizing, as Condition Four puts it, "the joyous fulfillment of a rounded life."

The Last Third Club has been called group therapy, but we soon hit on another name for it: friendship. As we went over the Conditions together, one a week for week after week, we came to know one another a bit. With knowledge came understanding, with understanding respect, and with respect that special kind of affection called friendship.

To sum up, the Conditions gradually became part of my daily life and habitual thought. I give a special priority to Condition One, the reminder that being in the last third of life makes one different from the general run. Condition Two always gives me a lift with its lesson that the so-called Grim Reaper is not really grim. Condition Seven, the going over one's life situation with friends, becomes a genuinely rewarding adventure in friendship. Conditions Eight through Ten keep my mind vigorous and alive through an unending sequence of new intellectual and spiritual discoveries. And Condition Twelve caps the lot with its call to action: we have a pearl of great value, but we can't keep it unless we pass it on.

Notes

Introduction

1. C. G. Jung, *Modern Man in Search of a Soul* (New York: Harcourt, Brace & Co., 1933; Harvest Book HB 2), p. 108.
2. Ibid., p. 109.

Chapter 1

1. C. G. Jung, *Modern Man in Search of a Soul* (New York: Harcourt, Brace & Co., 1933; Harvest Book HB 2), pp. 96-97. Used by permission of Harcourt, Brace, Jovanovich.
2. Ibid., p. 109.

Chapter 6

1. Henry David Thoreau, *The Variorum Walden*, ed. Walter Harding (Philadelphia: Washington Square Press, 1963), p. 7.
2. Walt Whitman, *Complete Poetry and Selected Prose*, ed. James E. Miller, Jr. (Boston: Houghton Mifflin Riverside Edition A 34, 1959), p. 25.

Chapter 8

1. C. G. Jung, *Memories, Dreams, Reflections* (New York: Random House, Pantheon Books, 1961), p. 325. Used by permission.
2. John White, ed., *The Highest State of Consciousness* (New York: Doubleday, Anchor book, 1972), pp. xiv, xvii.
3. Jung, *Memories, Dreams, Reflections*, p. 325.
4. William James, *Varieties of Religious Experience* (New York: Modern Library), p. 47.
5. C. G. Jung, *Modern Man in Search of a Soul* (New York: Harcourt, Brace & Co., 1933; Harvest Book HB 2), p. 240.
6. Jung, *Memories, Dreams, Reflections*, p. 359.
7. Raynor C. Johnson, *Nurslings of Immortality* (New York: Harper and Row, 1960), p. 46.

Chapter 10

1. Edgar D. Mitchell, "An Adventure in Consciousness," *Psychic Magazine*, Dec. 1972 (Vol. IV, No. 2), pp. 22 ff. Used by permission.

2. Charles T. Tart, "States of Consciousness and State-Specific Sciences," *Science*, June 16, 1972 (Vol. 176, No. 4040), p. 1210.

Chapter 11

1. Franz E. Winkler, *Man, the Bridge Between Two Worlds* (New York: Harper & Row, 1960) p. 18. Used by permission.
2. Ibid., p. 19.
3. Frank A. Brown, Jr., "The Rhythmic Nature of Animals and Plants," *Best Articles & Stories Magazine*, May 1960, p. 57.

Chapter 12

1. C. G. Jung, *Modern Man in Search of a Soul* (New York: Harcourt, Brace & Co., 1933; Harvest Book HB 2), pp. 108, 111. Used by permission.
2. Ibid., p. 103.
3. Ibid., pp. 102, 111.
4. Arthur Ford, *Unknown But Known* (New York: New American Library, Signet Book, 1968) p. 70.

FOR FURTHER READING

Basic

Bach, Marcus. *Major Religions of the World*. Nashville: Abingdon Press, 1970.

Bucke, R. M. *Cosmic Consciousness*. New York: E. P. Dutton.

Commoner, Barry. *Science and Survival*. New York: Ballantine Books, Inc., 1970.

Ford, Arthur. *The Life Beyond Death*. New York: Berkley Publishing Corp., 1972.

James, William. *Varieties of Religious Experience*. New York: New American Library, Mentor Book.

Jung, Carl G. *Modern Man in Search of a Soul*. New York: Harcourt Brace Jovanovich, Inc., Harvard Book.

May, Rollo. *Man's Search for Himself*. New York: W. W. Norton & Co., Inc.

Meadows, Donella H. *The Limits to Growth*. New York: Universe Books, 1972.

Smith, Alson. *Immortality: The Scientific Evidence*. New York: New American Library, Signet Book, 1967.

Smith, Bradford. *Meditation: The Inward Art*. Philadelphia: J. B. Lippincott, 1968.

Exploratory

Cummins, Geraldine. *The Road to Immortality*. Hackensack, N.J.: Wehman Brothers.

Eddy, Sherwood. *You Will Survive After Death*. New York: Holt, Rinehart & Winston, 1950.

Gardner, Adelaide. *Meditation: A Practical Study*. Wheaton, Ill.: Theosophical Publishing House, 1968.

Johnson, Raynor C. *The Imprisoned Splendor*. Wheaton, Ill.: Theosophical Publishing House.

Jung, Carl G. *Memories, Dreams, Reflections*. New York: Random House.

Karagulla, Shafica. *Breakthrough to Creativity*. Santa Monica, Calif.: De Vorss & Co.

King, Basil. *Conquest of Fear*. Hollywood, Calif.: Newcastle Publishing Co., Inc., 1972.

Kübler-Ross, Elisabeth. *On Death and Dying*. New York: Macmillan Company, 1970.

Osis, Karlis. *Deathbed Observations by Physicians*. New York: Parapsychology Foundation, Division of Research, 1961.

Sugrue, Thomas. *There Is a River*. New York: Dell Publishing Co.

Weatherhead, Leslie. *Life Begins at Death.* Nashville: Abingdon Press, 1970.

White, John (ed.). *The Highest State of Consciousness.* New York: Doubleday & Co., 1972.

Far Out

Brown, Rosemary. *Unfinished Symphonies.* New York: Bantam Books, Inc., 1972.

Castaneda, Carlos. *A Separate Reality.* New York: Simon & Schuster, Touchstone Paperback Service, 1972.

Ford, Arthur. *Unknown but Known.* New York: New American Library, 1969.

Monroe, Robert A. *Journeys Out of the Body.* New York: Doubleday & Co., 1971.

Pearce, Joseph C. *The Crack in the Cosmic Egg.* New York: Pocket Books, Inc., 1973.

White, Stewart Edward. *The Betty Book: Excursions into the World of Other Consciousness.* New York: E. P. Dutton.

Yogananda, Paramahansa. *Autobiography of a Yogi.* New York: Orientalia Inc.

Note: This list is, of course, only partial, and is in no sense "required reading," nor does The Last Third Club endorse any statement in any of these books. But the list includes some of the books we have found to be effective conversation-starters.

About the Author

Jerome Ellison, a native of Maywood, Illinois, has been an assistant editor of *Life*, associate editor of *Reader's Digest* from 1935-1942, editor-in-chief of *Liberty*, managing editor of *Collier's*, and editorial director of the U. S. Office of War Information, Bureau of Overseas Publications. He has taught at Indiana University and New Haven College and is a graduate of the University of Michigan, with an advanced degree from Southern Connecticut State College.

Mr. Ellison is an essayist, novelist, and literary critic whose published books include *The Run for Your Money*, *The Prisoner Ate a Hearty Breakfast*, *The Dam*, *John Brown's Soul*, *Report to the Creator*, *God on Broadway*, and *The Life Beyond Death* (with Arthur Ford). He now lives in Guilford, Connecticut, and is an enthusiastic member of The Last Third of Life Club, which has been renamed The Phenix Club.